Cambridge Elements

Elements in Indigenous Environmental Research

RESTORING INDIGENOUS PLACE NAMES

Making Anishinaabe Toponyms Visible Throughout the White Earth Ojibwe Reservation

Elan Pochedley
1855 Professor of Great Lakes Anishinaabe Knowledge, Spiritualities, and Cultural Practices, Michigan State University

CAMBRIDGE
UNIVERSITY PRESS

CAMBRIDGE
UNIVERSITY PRESS

Shaftesbury Road, Cambridge CB2 8EA, United Kingdom

One Liberty Plaza, 20th Floor, New York, NY 10006, USA

477 Williamstown Road, Port Melbourne, VIC 3207, Australia

314–321, 3rd Floor, Plot 3, Splendor Forum, Jasola District Centre, New Delhi – 110025, India

Cambridge University Press is part of Cambridge University Press & Assessment, a department of the University of Cambridge.

We share the University's mission to contribute to society through the pursuit of education, learning and research at the highest international levels of excellence.

www.cambridge.org
Information on this title: www.cambridge.org/9781009704571

DOI: 10.1017/9781009704564

When citing this work, please include a reference to the DOI 10.1017/9781009704564

First published 2026

A catalogue record for this publication is available from the British Library

A Cataloging-in-Publication data record for this Element is available from the Library of Congress

ISBN 978-1-009-70457-1 Hardback
ISBN 978-1-009-70460-1 Paperback
ISSN 2755-0826 (online)
ISSN 2755-0818 (print)

Restoring Indigenous Place Names

Making Anishinaabe Toponyms Visible Throughout the White Earth Ojibwe Reservation

Elements in Indigenous Environmental Research

DOI: 10.1017/9781009704564
First published online: April 2026

Elan Pochedley
Michigan State University

Author for correspondence: Elan Pochedley, pochedle@msu.edu

Abstract: This Element investigates the 2016 installation of Anishinaabemowin (Ojibwe language) toponym signs throughout the White Earth Reservation, reflecting an ongoing tradition of Ojibwe linguistic preservation rooted in environmental knowledge of waters. Drawing on ethnographic interviews with White Earth citizens, descendants, and personnel, this work addresses how these public markers make Anishinaabemowin visible in the world for Ojibwe youth and other White Earth Anishinaabeg while marking the reservation as an Ojibwe space. These place name signs, along with youth language programs, intervene in the legacy of imposed language loss of Anishinaabemowin on the White Earth Reservation caused by mission, day, and boarding schools. This Element examines Ojibwe people's intergenerational efforts to document place names, responses to these signs, and how they relate to toponymic authority and spatial belonging. This Element focuses on historic and contemporary stories of Ojibwe geographic relationships grounded in fishing, hunting, ricing, and gathering within and surrounding Gaa-waabaabiganikaag. This title is also available as open access on Cambridge Core.

Keywords: place names, Indigenous, geography, toponyms, Ojibwe

ISBNs: 9781009704571 (HB), 9781009704601 (PB), 9781009704564 (OC)
ISSNs: 2755-0826 (online), 2755-0818 (print)

Contents

Figure 1 Gaa-ode'iminkaag sign. Photo by author.

Figure 2 Sunset on Gaa-ode'iminkaag. Photo by author.

Introduction:
Restoring Indigenous Place Names in Settler Colonial Contexts

We want the Ojibwe on the top. We're not renaming something.

-Mary Otto (White Earth Ojibwe)[1]

Native storiers of survivance are prompted by natural reason, by a consciousness and sense of incontestable presence that arises from experiences in the natural

[1] Ross (2016).

world, the turn of seasons, sudden storms, migration of cranes, the ventures of tender lady's slippers, chance of moths overnight, unruly mosquitoes, and the favor of spirits in the water, rimy sumac, wild rice, thunder in the ice, bear, beaver, and faces in the stone.

-Gerald Vizenor (White Earth Ojibwe)[2]

Naming and Natural Reason: Anishinaabe Stories and Meanings of Place

The above quote by White Earth Ojibwe writer, scholar, and theorist Gerald Vizenor speaks to the significant role natural reason holds within expressions and pursuits of Indigenous survivance and Native presence. Vizenor's emphasis on natural reason is distinct from the romanticization and fetishization of Indigenous peoples' relationship with "nature," what the White Earth writer refers to as "nostalgia for animism in the commercial world."[3] Instead, in his work *Native Liberty*, Vizenor qualifies "natural reason" as being what undergirds Native survivance,[4] with the writer defining survivance as "an active sense of presence, the continuance of native stories, not a mere reaction, or a survivable name . . . Native survivance stories are renunciations of dominance, tragedy, and victimry."[5]

Throughout this Element, I address how the White Earth Nation's recent project of visibly restoring Ojibwe place names through road signs is rooted in ongoing Anishinaabe presence, as expressed in the endurance of these toponyms and the meanings embedded within them. This work chronicles how these road signs – in their inception, in the curation of names depicted, and in their relationship to youth language programs in Anishinaabemowin (i.e., the Anishinaabe language) – support the continuation of intergenerational knowledge exchanges while seeking to ensure that youth know their belonging on the White Earth Reservation. I examine how the curation of names for this signage project involved the practice of Ojibwe protocols, dialogic deliberation, and collective reasoning to effect the public markers. I trace how a cultural committee of the White Earth Nation (abbreviated WEN, also known as the White Earth Band of Ojibwe) curated these toponyms, their spellings, their meanings, and their translations. I argue that this recent initiative to preserve Ojibwe place names resonates with earlier efforts of the Ojibway-Dakota Research Society of Minnesota in the mid twentieth century.

This Element focuses on Ojibwe place name signs for bodies of water installed throughout Gaa-waabaabiganikaag – the White Earth Reservation – in 2016.

---

2 Vizenor (2009, p. 88). 3 Vizenor (2009, p. 10). 4 Vizenor (2009, pp. 88–89).
5 Vizenor (2009, p. 100).

These bilingual signs were created through the efforts of the White Earth Nation's Department of Education, in collaboration with the Minnesota Department of Transportation and with the financial support of the Minnesota Indian Affairs Council.[6] Mary Otto, the former Director of Education for the WEN, sought to create environmental print in the Ojibwe language so that Anishinaabe youth learning the language would see the language alive in the environment and world that they traveled through each day, as well as to encourage sense of Ojibwe pride and spatial belonging to Gaa-waabaabiganikaag. The Ojibwe name of the White Earth Reservation, Gaa-waabaabiganikaag, translates to "Land of the White Clay," in reference to the clay that lies beneath the soils of this place.[7] These road signs – in Mary's words – have been essential in

> "reclaiming and stating to our children that our language is alive, it's still alive, and it's a living thing, and that it should be all around us."[8]

In the aftermath of imposed language loss due to Indian boarding, mission, and day schools, these signs articulate the space of this reservation as home to the White Earth Anishinaabeg.[9]

The Ojibwe toponyms depicted on these road signs frequently convey observations, stories, or events that relate to specific places. These long-standing Anishinaabemowin place names speak to presences of or narratives concerning other-than-humans (e.g., strawberries, muskrats, pines, moose, bison/buffalo, and tullibee), the geological/physical/hydrological features of bodies of water or their surroundings ("many shore points," "small lake lying diagonally," "lake of islands," "round body of water," "body of water shape of elbow," "enclosed by steep bluff banks," "Graying Clay Earth Lake," and "two lakes together"), and sonic observations of a place ("travelling sound of cracking ice"). These Ojibwe toponym signs for bodies of water intersect at the confluence of Native survivance (through ongoing and visible Anishinaabe presence/continuance) and natural reason (in these depicted place names being rooted in environmental observations, features, and connections) (see Figures 1 and 2).

In this Element, I argue that these signs are not *solely* representations of Anishinaabe descriptions of place in the form of names; they *also* invite senses of belong, of observing Gaa-waabaabiganikaag as Ojibwe space, of asking questions concerning the meanings of the words inscribed on sheet aluminum,

---

6 *Anishinaabeg Today* (2016, p. 1).

7 Note: Gaa-waabaabiganikaag means the "Land of the White Clay" or "Place Name Marker/White Clay/Lots Of" in Ojibwemowin, being the Anishinaabe name for the White Earth Reservation. Sources: *Anishinaabeg Today* (2021, p. 3); McDougall (n.d.); Molin (1983, p. xi); and, White Earth Reservation Curriculum Committee et al. (1989, p. 27).

8 "Interview with Mary Otto," interview virtually conducted by Elan Pochedley, July 22, 2021.

9 White Earth Reservation Curriculum Committee et al. (1989, pp. 20, 28–31, 33–35).

and of intentionally bringing the Anishinaabe language and associated environmental knowledge to the public realm. This text theorizes the role of Ojibwe toponyms within Anishinaabe worldviews, while focusing on how generations of Ojibwe people have actively preserved, curated, and publicly shared these place names. While this Element's principal focus is on investigating the enduring life and significance of these toponyms, it is critically important to note that *the White Earth Nation's Department of Education and cultural committee created these signs specifically to ensure that Ojibwe youth feel pride in being Anishinaabe and understand that they belong at Gaa-waabaabiganikaag.* These road signs with Anishinaabemowin names for different bodies of water represent Ojibwe geographical knowledge and place-based connections, with this environmental print also cultivating spatial belonging for Ojibwe youth learning the language of their people and their ancestors.

Signing an Enduring Ojibwe Presence at White Earth

When I reached the boundaries of the White Earth Reservation for the first time in July 2017, I drove past a highway marker indicating that I was about to enter the reservation. I had grown used to these signs marking the original boundaries of treaty-constructed spaces in Oklahoma during times I've visited and worked for the Citizen Potawatomi Nation. What I did not anticipate, once within the boundaries of the White Earth Reservation, was the regular appearance of signs in Anishinaabemowin that displayed original Ojibwe place names of lakes and a river. These toponyms had been spoken, shared, and recorded across generations – in the minds of Anishinaabe people, in reports by the Ojibway-Dakota Research Society, and, recently, on the road signs.

With the White Earth Reservation being a site of intense dispossession for Ojibwe people, these signs throughout Gaa-waabaabiganikaag visually disrupt legacies of state-sanctioned territorial expropriation that have been well documented.[10] To put into Vizenor-ian terms, these signs – in their presentation of the Anishinaabe language and in their conveyance of ongoing Ojibwe geographical knowledge – present a mode and platform for "resistance to absence, . . . tragedy, nihility, and victimry."[11] I suggest that in order to comprehend what's accomplished through these markers' visible interventions in the landscape of the reservation, one must understand the relationship between territorial usurpation and environmental change at White Earth. With these Ojibwe names largely referring to historic locations of plants and animals, physical features of waters, and sonic emergences throughout Gaa-waabaabiganikaag, these signs visually present enduring Ojibwe geographic

[10] Meyer (1999). [11] Vizenor (2009, p. 1).

and environmental knowledges in a context of settler colonial dislocation and dispossession. The concept of "settler colonialism" addressed throughout this Element refers to territorial, relational, ecological, and/or linguistic disruptions, displacements, and dispossessions experienced by Ojibwe people and the WEN. My use of this concept is informed by Kyle Whyte's definition: "Settler colonialism refers to complex social processes in which at least one society seeks to move permanently onto the terrestrial, aquatic, and aerial places lived in by one or more other societies who already derive economic vitality, cultural flourishing, and political self-determination from the relationships they have established with the plants, animals, physical entities, and ecosystems of those places."[12]

The usurpation of Ojibwe territory throughout the reservation can largely be attributed to predatory allotment policies and mortgaging practices during the late nineteenth and twentieth centuries,[13] as well as the seizing of lands due to the illegal taxation of Ojibwe people.[14] Jean O'Brien, in reflecting on her grandma's writings on Ojibwe land loss at Gaa-waabaabiganikaag, chronicles how the dispossession of the Anishinaabeg was facilitated through the nexus of federal Indian allotment policy (implemented under the 1889 Nelson Act), the 1906 Clapp Rider (which supposedly cleared trust restrictions on the sale of many Ojibwe allotments), land speculation by Euro-Americans, and the extraction of resources by the lumber industry.[15] On the scale of transferred titles from Ojibwe to Euro-American owners during the early decades of the reservation, O'Brien states: " … by 1909, an Indian Office investigation revealed that 80 percent of White Earth allotments had passed out of Indian hands, spurring a flurry of further investigations and lawsuits over wrongful dispossession that still have not been fully settled."[16] The 1977 court case *State vs. Zay Zah* further demonstrated the scope of fraud and coercion at White Earth leading to the dispossession of Ojibwe people, with the Minnesota Supreme Court ruling that "removal of the U.S. government's trust responsibility under the 1889 Nelson Act should not have occurred unless the allottee *applied* for such removal."[17]

Numerous White Earth Anishinaabe scholars have written extensively on the structural impacts of land dispossession and the territorial usurpation by Euro-Americans at Gaa-waabaabiganikaag, including Winona LaDuke and Jill Doerfler.[18] In the foreword of Ignatia Broker's novel *Night Flying Woman*,

[12] Whyte (2017, p. 165).

[13] "Interview with Jacob Syverson," interview virtually conducted by Elan Pochedley, July 12, 2021.

[14] White Earth Reservation Curriculum Committee et al. (1989, p. 37); and, Child (2012, p. 141).

[15] O'Brien (2017, pp. 349, 355–356, 359–360, 364).

[16] O'Brien (2017, pp. 355–356).

[17] Meyer (1999, p. 230, emphasis in original); and, Minnesota Supreme Court (1977).

[18] Doerfler (2015, pp. 1–30).

Paulette Fairbanks Molin writes, "Before the allotment policy ended in the 1930s, two-thirds of the Indian land in the United States had passed into white hands. The effects on the White Earth Reservation were devastating. By 1971, only 4 per cent of the original reservation was Indian-owned trust land; another 4 per cent was 'marginal land' purchased for the Indians under the New Deal's Farm Security Administration program."[19] LaDuke describes the environmental consequences of the Ojibwe's dispossession for the lands and forests of Gaawaabaabiganikaag, as well as their impacts on the Anishinaabe people who relied on the woodlands for their health and survival: "The stripping of the great forests of White Earth began a process that would be devastating to the Anishinaabeg forest culture. Great maple trees and maple sugarbushes moved horizontally toward logging mills, clear-cuts replaced biodiverse groves of medicinal plants and trees, basket-makers searched for materials, and birch-bark canoe-makers couldn't find the huge trees for the great Anishinaabeg canoes."[20] Despite the legacy of rampant dispossession and deforestation at White Earth, the recently installed Anishinaabemowin signs provide a visual backdrop of Ojibwe presence constantly appearing, passing, and emerging once more while traveling across the reservation.

The Medicine Chest: Abundance in a Context of Dispossession

Despite histories of displacement, of land theft, and of resource extraction leading to environmental desecration, the abundance of life at Gaawaabaabiganikaag has remained firmly articulated by citizens and personnel of the White Earth Nation. In an interview with Jacob Syverson (White Earth Ojibwe), the WEN Land Analyst, he described the diversity of lakes found within the reservation: "We've got a lot of those 'valley lakes,' is what I call them. Lake of the Valley, Bad Medicine Lake, Juggler Lake; those big hundred-foot hole lakes. And then once you go down the hill, then you get all those nice little shallow lakes. It's so diverse, you know. It's one of the most valuable reservations . . ."[21] Diversity of land features is not restricted to bodies of water. In a 2017 interview, Doug McArthur (White Earth Ojibwe), the nation's Wildlife Manager, shared how the reservation is home to three biomes:

> The most unique thing about White Earth is that we reside in three biomes. So we have the Prairie Biome out here. Then we have the transitional Deciduous right in the middle. So you look east here, you'll start going up a hill, and

[19] Molin (1983, p. xii). [20] LaDuke (1999, p. 120).

[21] "Interview with Jacob Syverson," interview virtually conducted by Elan Pochedley, July 12, 2021, p. 34.

> that's kind of our transition zone into that. And then the east side was traditionally Pine/Coniferous Forest.[22]

I am grateful to Doug for introducing me to the place name signs in Anishinaabemowin, while also sharing knowledge of the great diversity that defines the environments and ecosystems throughout Gaa-waabaabiganikaag.

The numerous biomes, forests, waters, and other-than-human relatives of Gaa-waabaabiganikaag have enabled the Ojibwe to continue practicing ancestral lifeways within the reservation, while supporting the perpetual renewal of Anishinaabe people's relationships with specific foods and medicines across generations. In a 1993 speech, LaDuke described Gaa-waabaabiganikaag as "the medicine chest of the Ojibways," stating,

> We have wild rice, we have deer, we have beaver, we have fish – every food we need. On the eastern part of the reservation there are stands of white pine. On the part farthest west there used to be buffalo, but this area is now farmland, situated in the Red River Valley. That is our area, the land reserved to us under treaty.[23]

This articulation of flourishing plants, animals, and trees throughout the reservation resonates with an early history of White Earth authored by Julia Ann Warren Spears in 1907. Spears, the first teacher at a government school on the White Earth Reservation[24] and the sister of Ojibwe historian William Whipple Warren, provided the following description of Gaa-waabaabiganikaag during the summer and fall of 1868 – the first year that a group of Ojibwe migrants from Crow Wing had relocated to White Earth following the establishment of the reservation:

> . . . there was plenty of wild rice in the lakes, and ducks, geese and prairie chickens were also plentiful. The lakes were filled with many varieties of fish, including catfish, pickerel, muskallonge [*sic*], black and rock bass, suckers, red-horse and wall-eyed pike. Sturgeon were also caught in White Earth Lake. The first two years deer were quite plentiful, and also elk, moose, bear, muskrats, and rabbits.[25]

The abundance of biodiverse life at Gaa-waabaabiganikaag is further described and contextualized within Anishinaabe worldviews in a history published through the Minnesota Chippewa Tribe, entitled *White Earth: A History* (1989). Members of the White Earth Reservation Curriculum Committee provide the following reverential description of this place, the presences of other-than-humans, and the plentiful waters found throughout the reservation:

[22] "Interview with Doug McArthur," interview conducted by Elan Pochedley, White Earth Reservation, July 18, 2017.

[23] LaDuke (1993). [24] Wilcox (1907, pp. 225, 255). [25] Spears (1907, pp. 247–248).

> Long ago Kitchi Manido created the world, and White Earth is still one of the loveliest parts of his creation. It is a land of lakes, streams, and marshes covered with cattails and wild rice. It is a land of aspen, evergreen, and maple, providing food and shelter for the slow-footed muskrat and the swift white-tailed deer. It is a land of quiet and incredible beauty.[26]

While the Ojibwe people of White Earth have dealt with rampant dispossession, corrupt land speculation practices, and harmful environmental changes, the enduring flourishing of life that characterizes the reservation has remained in the memories and often in the realities of the Anishinaabe people of Gaa-waabaabiganikaag.

Anishinaabe Aki / Ojibwe Territory: Environments of Relations

Anishinaabe people have historically and often contemporarily practiced their own forms of place-based relationships and property systems that regulate who has access and obligations to specific harvesting sites. Michael Witgen elaborates on this point in his discussion of territoriality within Anishinaabewaki (aka "Anishinaabe aki") prior to the reservation period of the mid nineteenth century. Witgen offers a definition and conceptualization of Anishinaabe territory, writing, "In the indigenous west, and even on the middle ground, space was not bounded by social identity, or by the national structure of European political formations. Kinship, and its attendant obligations, determined access and exclusivity to the physical world-fish runs, animals, wild rice, etc. – and to spatialized social formations such as villages, hunting territories, trade routes, etc."[27] Witgen conveys how permission to harvest (e.g., seasonal hunting, fishing, ricing, and gathering) in specific locations was contingent on following land/water-use protocols, respecting Anishinaabe forms of relationality and property, and recognizing and fulfilling obligations. The legacy – and sometimes endurance – of Anishinaabe aki as territory structured and bounded by kinship partially informs the foci of this Element. The Ojibwe toponyms addressed in these pages hold meanings associated with environmental observations, physical features of bodies of water, other-than-human presences, and storied landscapes.

Mobility and cyclical returns were, and often remain, critical to the realization of an Ojibwe country defined by spatial relationships and kinship. Brenda Child elaborates on how the Anishinaabeg's seasonal migrations were determined by the emergences and lifecycles of plants and animals, while Ojibwe approaches for dividing labor supported an equitable society that largely

---

[26] White Earth Reservation Curriculum Committee et al. (1989, p. 3).

[27] Witgen (2011, p. 395).

revolved around women's expertise, leadership roles, governance, and property rights:[28] " . . . Ojibwe people in the Great Lakes region did not live or conduct politics within the confines of a bounded geographic space but, rather, seasonally moved within their homelands, returning every year to the best places for gathering, farming, fishing, hunting, making maple sugar, and harvesting wild rice."[29] She notes that these seasonal activities and annual geographic returns connected Ojibwe people to their other-than-human relatives and specific sites for harvests.[30] In 1989, the White Earth Reservation Curriculum Committee described the regular renewal of place-based relationships with hunting/fishing/gathering sites, family returns to their respective sugar bush locations each spring, property claims being marked in wild rice beds, and the inheritance of hunting spots.[31] Their collective scholarship illustrates how Ojibwe seasonal harvests and associated migrations are expressions of Anishinaabe territoriality, governance, kinship, law, and property systems.

Gaa-waabaabiganikaag is found within a small portion of historic Anishinaabe aki. Kinship obligations, seasonal harvests, and geographic returns continue to hold significance to many Ojibwe people of White Earth, as they have for generations. This demonstrates the endurance of certain relational logics, ethics, practices, and principles that undergird(ed) the governing structures of Anishinaabewaki, as defined by Child and Witgen, which will be illustrated through ethnographic interviews in the conclusion. I assert that the visible presence of Anishinaabemowin toponyms also reflects enduring Ojibwe geographic relationships throughout Gaa-waabaabiganikaag, despite legacies and realities of dispossession within the reservation's borders. These signs mark the endurance of Ojibwe spatial presences, environmental knowledge, and language, in these markers being located across different bodies of water with descriptive names written in Anishinaabemowin. I argue that the presence of these signs pushes against settler colonial projects of cultural assimilation, land dispossession, and spatial confinement that have impacted generations of Ojibwe people. The WEN cultural committee's intention in installing these signs was to make sure that youth are proud to be Ojibwe and see their language alive in their environment. In addition, *I* suggest that these markers – in their very existence – trouble the primacy of imposed English place names and property boundaries across Gaa-waabaabiganikaag. By sharing place names

[28] Child (2012, pp. 39, 48, 63–64, 96, 102–103). [29] Child (2012, pp. 29–30).
[30] Child (2012, pp. 63–64).
[31] White Earth Reservation Curriculum Committee et al. (1989, pp. 13, 16–17).

rooted in the ancestral memories, movements, and presences of Anishinaabe people throughout their homelands and homewaters, these signs demonstrate White Earth Ojibwe survivance – of language, of spatial belonging, and of inherited geographic knowledge.

1 Ojibwe Place Names: Geographic Belonging and the Lives of Anishinaabe Toponyms

What is encapsulated within a place name? What defines a people's or nation's territory? What is the relationship between spatial belonging, authority, and toponyms? How do place names communicate spatial histories and relationships? Memories of place? Ecologies past, present, or future? And how do they connect people to place? These are a few of the questions that guide this investigation into the impetus, curation, and installation of the Ojibwe toponym signs on the White Earth Reservation, as well as people's responses to these markers.

Throughout this Element, I examine the role toponymic authority – or the authority to name environmental presences – played in the White Earth Nation making Ojibwe place names visible throughout Gaa-waabaabiganikaag in 2016. *To understand how toponymic authority operated in relation to this Anishinaabemowin signage projects for waters throughout Gaa-waabaabiganikaag, I examine (1) from where the authority to name is derived; (2) from where historic toponyms and their meanings are found; (3) how naming protocols (such as the collective curation of names) were practiced; (4) how these signs intervene in legacies and everyday realities of the suppression of Anishinaabemowin and the dispossession of reservation lands; and, (5) what collaborations were cultivated to create these signs inscribed with Ojibwe toponyms.*

In this Element, I argue that these signs communicate an endurance of Ojibwe presence, language, and environmental relationships concerning Gaa-waabaabiganikaag across generations. I posit that the continuance of this knowledge reflects an enduring Ojibwe presence despite legacies of dispossession, of both territory and language. As addressed in upcoming sections, this is evident in the labor, recordings, deliberations, reports, and initiatives of the Ojibway-Dakota Research Society of Minnesota and the White Earth cultural committee who recently created these markers. Despite legacies and enduring consequences of attempted cultural, linguistic, and territorial elimination, the efforts of Ojibwe people have kept alive and now made publicly visible these place names. This section investigates what these toponyms mean to Anishinaabe people, focusing on how the restoration of place names has been and may be understood within Anishinaabe worldviews by drawing on the contributions of knowledge-sharers, scholars, and writers.

This Element's focus on the *restoration* and *preservation* of Ojibwe place names refers to a combination of restorative methodologies recently employed by the White Earth Nation, as well as practiced by other Anishinaabe people and nations across generations. *Restoration in the context of this Element refers to the process of identifying, curating, translating, and publicly displaying Indigenous place names. Restoring, in the sense employed here, concerns not the act of returning that which has entirely disappeared, but rather refers to the process of gathering and representing knowledge of toponyms that have been retained across generations, stored in the memories of Anishinaabe people or archived in reports wherein Ojibwe people's geographic knowledge has been recorded.*

Toponyms and Naming from Anishinaabe Perspectives

In *Dancing on Our Turtle's Back*, Leanne Simpson draws attention to the Otonabee River coursing through the territory of the Michi Saagiig Nishnaabeg. Simpson notes the name of the river "is spoken by people who have no idea what the word means, and who are ignorant of both the history of this Michi Saagiig Nishnaabeg land they live on, as well as our contemporary Michi Saagiig Nishnaabeg presence." Simpson refers to this as a "disappearance of Indigenous presence," as expressed in non-Native Canadians' retention and regular recitation of a Nishnaabeg place name without comprehending the meaning of Otonabee, paired with the public's lack of awareness of these Nishnaabeg people's presence historically and contemporarily. She discusses how Elder Gidigaa Migizi (Doug Williams) presented a translation distinct from the one found on Wikipedia, which translated the Otonabee River's Nishnaabeg name – "Odoonabii-Ziibi" – to the "Tulibee River." Simpson writes:

> [Gidigaa Migizi] began by telling me that the first part means 'heart,' coming from the word *ode*; and the word *odemgat* means boiling water, because when water boils, it looks like the bubbling or beating of a heart. He then explained that Otonabee is an anglicized version of Odenabe – the river that beats like a heart in reference to the bubbling and boiling waters of the rapids along the river.[32]

The translation offered to Simpson by their Elder and teacher is rooted in Nishnaabeg linguistic knowledge and worldviews, adding depth to the meaning of the river's name. We can deduce that the name itself is rooted in observations of the river, based on Gidigaa Migizi's description. In a sense, the river embodied and therefore communicated its own name to the Nishnaabeg.

I suggest that this relates to the story of Nanabozho's early journey wherein he built relationships with and learned the names of all forms of life on Turtle

[32] Simpson (2011, pp. 93–94).

Island. Nanabozho is a protagonist in many Anishinaabe stories that teaches lessons. Robin Kimmerer shares a story of Nanabozho's travels after being "placed on the Earth" to learn the names of plants, trees, and animals who "were already living there in harmony with one another." Kimmerer illustrates the relationship between Nanabozho learning the gifts of other-than-human beings and their respective names through listening and visiting with these relatives:

> He was given the responsibility of . . . learning from them what gifts they had to share with the people who would be coming. Every plant he encountered taught him of its worth, the ways its roots could be eaten, the medicines it made, how its bark was ready to become lodges, its branches baskets, its berries food to sweeten life. As Nanabozho came to know and respect each plant, he also came to know their names.[33]

In this Anishinaabe story shared by a Potawatomi environmental scientist, Nanabozho, the one who was to learn the names of the abundant living beings throughout Turtle Island, had to first build healthy interspecies relationships with the other-than-humans of this place.[34]

How does the ability to understand deeper meanings embedded in Indigenous place names inform relationships with and belonging to specific places or bodies of water? Simpson addresses what differentiates her experience from non-Native Canadians in witnessing this river's name, writing, "When I hear or read the word 'Otonabee,' I think 'Odenabe,' and I am immediately connected to a physical place within my territory and a space where my culture communicates a multi-layered and nuanced meaning that is largely unseen and unrecognized by non-Indigenous peoples." Simpson observes that perceiving this name pulls her into "a Nishnaabeg presence" rooted in the philosophy, stories, knowledges, and spatial connections of her people, the Michi Saagiig Nishnaabeg. She writes, "Nishnaabemowin seamlessly joins my body to the body of my first mother; it links my beating heart to the beating river that flows through my city."[35] Here, Simpson articulates the ways that the presence, evocation, and understanding of Nishnaabeg place names reflects and reifies bonds of Nishnaabeg spatial belonging while summoning connections to her people's territories, language, and knowledges.

I suggest that the recognition of inherited spatial relationships to place through comprehension of the deep meanings of Nishnaabeg toponyms, as described by Simpson, resonates with the scholarship of Lawrence Gross on stories and their roles in transferring and renewing place-based relationships across generations. Gross attends to the "affective nature of storytelling," focusing on the interplay between the environments described in Anishinaabe

[33] Kimmerer (2017, p. 375). [34] Kimmerer (2017, p. 375). [35] Simpson (2011, p. 95).

stories and the building of spatial relationships.[36] Gross writes: "... elements of the natural world take on meaningful associations drawn from and inspired by Anishinaabe stories ... the stories also come alive because the Anishinaabeg are in contact with the characters in the stories ... there is a mutually reinforcing dynamic at work in which the stories and elements of the natural world imbue each other with meaning and emotion."[37] The White Earth Anishinaabe scholar emphasizes the significance of stories and place-based experiences within Anishinaabe aki for Ojibwe youth, with knowledge sharers teaching these stories and encouraging place-based experiences such as sugaring, fishing, hunting, harvesting manoomin, and fasting. Gross asserts that this ensures that Anishinaabe youth continue to hold and renew ancestral bonds with their other-than-human relatives, as well as their homelands and homewaters.[38]

Anishinaabe toponyms can reference stories of people's relationships with specific places that may refer to stewardship practices, harvesting or spiritual sites, geologic or hydrologic formations, or presences of other-than-humans. For example, Gidigaa Migizi shares the meaning of Pamitaashkodeyong, otherwise known as Rice Lake, within the territory of the Michi Saagiig Nishnaabeg: "[Pamitaashkodeyong] means 'where it burns and where it travels' because our people used to burn the south shore of Rice Lake to maintain a mishkode – a meadow or a prairie."[39] Here, this toponym refers to a practice of the Nishnaabeg of this region that relates to Indigenous environmental interactions, knowledge, and stewardship with fire. Through the writings of Simpson, Gross, Kimmerer, and Gidigaa Migizi, we can begin to understand how Anishinaabe place names, stories, environmental observations, and geographic belonging are interrelated, demonstrating the significance of the presence, articulation, observation, and comprehension of Ojibwe toponyms in Anishinaabemowin across generations.

Intergenerational Geographic Knowledge, Restorative Methods, and Spatial Belonging

Indigenous Studies scholarship has examined the myriad ways Indigenous peoples' homelands, homewaters, and environmental relationships have been "mapped over." Prior to beginning a canoe journey tracing familial hunting and harvesting sites, Madeline Whetung records experiencing anxiety concerning her ability to experience connections with her Nishnaabeg ancestors due to the density of the colonialscape of southern Ontario: "I was worried that the built up settler geography all around me would have obscured our presence so

[36] Gross (2014, p. 155). [37] Gross (2014, p. 156).
[38] Gross (2014, pp. 59–63, 74–75, 156–157, 160–166). [39] Gidigaa Migizi (2018, p. 32).

completely that I would be unable to feel our own landscape."[40] Drawing on Sarah Hunt's concept of the "colonialscape," Whetung addresses myriad ways that Michi Saagiig Nishnaabeg spaces have become mapped over: the jurisdiction of lands surrounding waterways being restructured through systems of private property and exclusive ownership – restricting Nishnaabeg mobility and seasonal migrations; sites of preexisting Nishnaabeg presence being marked with Canadian nationalist symbols and discourses; imposed manipulations of waterways occurring without the consent of the Michi Saagiig Nishnaabeg; and, the ways these restructurings render Nishnaabeg appearances and migrations as interruptions to an otherwise *seemingly* settled landscape.[41] I suggest that we can draw on Whetung's theorizations regarding the obscuring of Indigenous presences (e.g., Native peoples' and nations' environmental relations, spatial histories, place-based authorities, and modes of relationality) to interpret the significance of interventions made by the appearance of Anishinaabemowin place names throughout the White Earth Reservation.

Whetung effectively communicates that restoring Indigenous presences throughout respective nations' homewaters and homelands may revolve around realizing what memories have endured across generations while developing methods for publicly practicing or sharing this knowledge in ways that interrupt narratives and myths of Native absence. Whetung concludes the chronicle of her journey with the following realizations:

> By going out on the land, and learning from it in creative ways, we can access all the knowledge that our ancestors have stowed away here for us. These lessons will help us move forward as a nation, and keep Nishnaabeg geographies alive ... My paddling experience made me believe our land-based movements can connect us across the boundaries of settler society to the ancestors that are there waiting.[42]

Describing the stakes of her research, Whetung writes: "This thesis is about how Nishnaabeg geographical knowledge can be brought to life in the contemporary colonialscape, and the continuity of the Indigenous landscape in my home territory."[43]

In this Element, I suggest that the Anishinaabemowin signs publicly center Ojibwe geographic and environmental knowledge in impactful ways, while the constellation of bilingual road signs featuring Anishinaabemowin toponyms marks the White Earth Reservation as a place of Ojibwe roots and relationships. In Section 2, I address how the attempted elimination of Ojibwe linguistic presences in assimilatory residential, mission, and day schools relates to the

[40] Whetung (2016, p. 93). [41] Whetung (2016, pp. 90–111).
[42] Whetung (2016, pp. 109–111). [43] Whetung (2016, p. 91).

intention behind creating these road signs: to ensure that Ojibwe youth are proud of being Anishinaabe and that they see their language as "alive," as "a living thing . . . that should be all around us" (to quote Mary Otto).[44] In breath being of critical significance within Anishinaabe stories of creation and migration,[45] the visual presence of Ojibwe language through the signs is interrelated with the White Earth Nation's contemporary youth education efforts concerning the vocal return of Anishinaabemowin throughout the lands of Gaa-waabaabiganikaag.[46] In creating "environmental print" (Mary's terminology) in the Ojibwe language, waters marked by these signs are sites where oral, aural, and textual expressions of Anishinaabemowin are becoming re-assembled, re-articulated, and observed throughout the White Earth Reservation.

A related example of the intergenerational preservation, recording, and enunciation of Anishinaabe place names is presented by Leanne Simpson. Simpson describes a project in which Anishinaabe Elders from the Long Lake #58 Reserve mapped their place names and relationships to land, with the intention that this "land-use atlas" would enable policymakers to "use the information to minimize the impacts of development on our lands and ways of life." Simpson describes the resulting map as a translation of Elders' geographic and environmental knowledge "into a form that would be *recognized* by industry and the state." She posits that Elders may have desired to participate in the project to collectively create "a tool to generate cohesion, pride, and rebuilding within our own communities when our own people saw visually and so clearly what dispossession, displacement, encroachment, and industrial extractivism look like over our territories across time."[47] While locations and histories of violence and environmental desecration were also chronicled, the documenting of toponyms shared by the Long Lake #58 Elders created a map of relationships.[48] Simpson describes how the recorded Anishinaabe toponyms – "hundreds and hundreds of names" – referred to locations of significance: places of life, of harvests, of hunts, of traplines, of medicines, of migrations, of other-than-humans, of spirituality, of death, and of promises.[49] This project created a written record of Anishinaabe people's environmental relationships, geographic knowledge, patterns of mobility, and lived spatial connections. As discussed in Section 3, the White Earth cultural committee relied on the toponyms recorded in reports by the Ojibway-Dakota Research Society of Minnesota from the 1940s and 1950 when creating the recently installed Anishinaabemowin signs (as compiled and published in 1963 by Karen

[44] "Interview with Mary Otto," interview virtually conducted by Elan Pochedley, July 22, 2021.
[45] Benton-Banai (1988/2010, pp. 2–4). [46] *Anishinaabeg Today* (2022, p. 9).
[47] Simpson (2017, pp. 12–13). [48] Simpson (2017, p. 15). [49] Simpson (2017, p. 14).

Daniels Petersen). While reasons and intentions for recording Indigenous place names may vary across contexts, these examples demonstrate Anishinaabe people intentionally documenting their place-based relationships, with toponyms being a prioritized focus for archiving and representing Ojibwe presence and geographic knowledge.

The language of restoration employed in this text is also informed by Robin Kimmerer's theorization of "biocultural restoration." Kimmerer writes, "Biocultural restoration raises the bar for environmental quality of the reference ecosystem, so that as we care for the land, it can once again care for us," wherein "reconnecting people and the landscape" is critical."[50] I suggest that the public presence and awareness of Anishinaabe toponyms is directly related to supporting Anishinaabe people's ongoing relationships with places of relational and ecological importance: locations and environments where their stories have occurred and sometimes continue to unfold, as well as sites known by the presences of their relatives, the shapes of waters, or particular sounds. Environmental records are embedded in many of the place names of Gaa-waabaabiganikaag and its surroundings, with toponyms being one way in which memories of other-than-humans' presences and Ojibwe relationships to place are retained. For example, Mashkode bizhiki ziibi (Buffalo River) is a waterway historically marked by the presence of Buffalo herds that no longer unrestrictedly roam the prairies of Gaa-waabaabiganikaag or other areas east of the Red River. In 1907, local historian Alvin H. Wilcox presented evidence of bison at White Earth during an 1848 Ojibwe hunt, within nineteenth-century journal entries referring to their presence, and through references of their remains found along the Buffalo River by those conducting government surveys.[51] The visual representation of the Ojibwe name for this river – Mashkode bizhiki ziibi – combines the knowledge of bison's historic presence with long-standing Ojibwe geographic connections to this river that flows through Gaa-waabaabiganikaag. Historic maps of the region include Dakota, Ojibwe, and English names for this body of water: "Katapa Watpa" and "Buffalo R[iver]" in Giacomo Beltrami's 1827 map,[52] "Buffaloe River" in James Allen's 1832 map,[53] and "Pijihi or Buffalo R." in Joseph Nicollet's 1843 map.[54] The Ojibway-Dakota Research Society's sixth report (1950) concludes with a note describing deliberations concerning "Pijihi," whether it was a Dakota or Ojibwe name, and its possible meanings. The report's authors note "'Pijihi' is a Sioux [Dakota] word meaning hay and conceiveably [*sic*] ... a name for a place of forage for Buffalo," while "the word Pijihi may have

[50] Kimmerer (2013, p. 338). [51] Wilcox (1907, pp. 44–55). [52] Beltrami (1827, map).
[53] Allen (1832, map). [54] Nicollet et al. (1843, map).

been a misunderstanding by settlers or explorers of the Ojibway syllables 'bishiki' meaning 'cow' and understood by them to mean 'buffalo'" – with "'Mushkodaybishiki' meaning 'Prairie Ox or Cow'" [i.e. bison] in Anishinaabemowin.[55] Without acknowledging a source, Rev. Chrysostom Verwyst presented the name "Pijikiwi Sibi" in Anishinaabemowin for the Buffalo River in a 1916 glossary.[56] Regardless of whose name was inscribed on Nicollet's map, the legacy of bison along its shores and historic Indigenous place name(s) for the waterway demonstrate that this river was marked by the presences of the pte/tataŋka/mashkode bizhiki, Dakota, and Ojibwe. The "Mashkode bizhiki ziibi" sign installed by the White Earth Nation visibly signifies the endurance of Ojibwe connections to the river's waters, while present-day bison restoration programs by the White Earth Nation[57] and Dakota nations[58] demonstrate ongoing relationships, obligations, and mutual reciprocity with this other-than-human relative.

In Section 3, I demonstrate how the WEN cultural committee practiced a form of restorative cartography through the curation and visual representation of Ojibwe toponyms, relying on the previous efforts of Anishinaabeg from White Earth and elsewhere who collaborated with Dakota people through the Minneapolis-based Ojibway-Dakota Research Society. I associate "restorative cartography" with "utilizing archival sources in unconventional ways to illuminate Indigenous presences and networks of relationality."[59] Ojibwe mobility between the Twin Cities and Gaa-waabaabiganikaag was critical for the development of the original place name reports in the mid twentieth century, with the society's co-founders William Madison and Joseph Fairbanks being originally from the White Earth Reservation.[60] A member of the WEN cultural committee, the late Leonard "Sonny" McDougall encouraged a focus on Ojibwe names for bodies of water, recalling having previously seen a work of Ojibwe toponyms in the Twin Cities. Mary Otto supported the signs primarily focusing on lakes and a river of the reservation due to water's significance to Anishinaabe people, with Otto later locating the report mentioned by Sonny.[61] While the responses of White Earth Ojibwe citizens and personnel to the signs demonstrate a lack of familiarity with these Anishinaabe toponyms prior to their installation, Ojibwe people's perceptions of these markers demonstrates that such efforts to make Ojibwe geographic knowledge visible are part of restoring Ojibwe presences

[55] Ojibway-Dakota Research Society of Minnesota (1950, *Report No. 6*).
[56] Verwyst (1916, p. 257). [57] *Anishinaabeg Today* (2024, p. 7).
[58] Olson (2023); Prairie Island Indian Community (n.d.); *WCCO CBS News Minnesota* (2023); and, Adler (2023).
[59] Pochedley (2021).
[60] Ojibway-Dakota Research Society of Minnesota (1945, *Report No. 2*, p. 12).
[61] "Interview with Mary Otto," interview virtually conducted by Elan Pochedley, July 22, 2021.

throughout the environment of Gaa-waaabaabiganikaag. Section 4 details how the emergence of environmental print in the Ojibwe language is a form of biocultural restoration, insofar as these roads signs for waters are encouraging the learning – and therefore endurance – of Ojibwe geographic knowledge and place names that are largely rooted in environmental observations and the presences of other-than-humans.

The Anishinaabemowin toponym signs at White Earth offer a critical medium for communicating intergenerational Ojibwe knowledge of place and spatial belonging. The signs are inherently textual, visual, and visible, uniquely engaging in Ojibwe literary traditions. Heid Erdrich, a Turtle Mountain Ojibwe poet and author, offers a powerful theorization of how Anishinaabe literary ancestors inform, influence, and mark the navigations of contemporary Ojibwe writers:

> The Anishinaabe word name' is a verb transitive animate and means to "find/ leave signs of somebody's presence." While engaging in research in order to recover an Ojibwe tradition of writing in English, I find landmarks of literature, signs of presence, and draw them toward my understanding of the Anishinaabe word name'. It seems apt: What helps us know a place? Landmarks. What helps us know a people? The marks/signs they leave, that we find. These marks and landmarks help us follow their path across a landscape of time . . . When we find what another leaves, we are connected across time . . . Name' is the perfect metaphor for the Anishinaabe poet-critic to employ in a search for literary ancestry. We follow our literary ancestors – not with a destination in mind, not with the intent to claim territory, but because we want to know who has gone before us, who now guides us. We take comfort in their signs of presence along our way.[62]

As will be addressed in Sections 2–4, these signs throughout White Earth mark the reservation as a space of Ojibwe belonging, history, and presence, while also supporting the ongoing life of Anishinaabemowin, a language traversing present, past, and future throughout Anishinaabe aki.

The signs ensure that place names known by ancestors of Ojibwe people at Gaa-waabaabiganikaag will continue to be witnessed, observed, and ideally spoken by present and future generations of White Earth Anishinaabeg. Erdrich ties together her theorization of name' with Gerald Vizenor's writing on survivance:

> Vizenor's survivance is drawn toward story as persistence and resistance, a postcolonial response as well as a tradition, and *name'* implies a being, a spirit, inherently present in the traces left, such as in the signs or writing. Both concepts suggest an Ojibwe-centered notion of literature as persistence

[62] Erdrich (2013, p. 14).

> and continuance, a presence that is at once new and at the same time based in an Ojibwe epistemology as old as petroglyphs.[63]

These public markers tie together the sonic with the textual, creating an interplay between ancestral memories of spoken toponyms, present-day signs featuring Ojibwe place names, and anticipated future generations of Ojibwe people familiar with these names, their meanings, and their language.

The place names of Gaa-waabaabiganikaag have traveled across generations, sometimes printed on early nineteenth-century maps and described in journals, at other times recorded in the reports of the Ojibway-Dakota Research Society of Minnesota in the 1940s and 1950s. Knowledge of these place names constitutes a unique form of Ojibwe intellectual ancestry concerning geography, toponyms, environmental observations, and, as demonstrated by the signs, spatial literature. I suggest that the literary ancestors of these Anishinaabemowin signs were previous generations of Ojibwe people who shared these names and their meanings with cartographers (e.g., Joseph Nicollet), with religious figures documenting Anishinaabe toponyms (e.g., reverends Joseph Gilfillan and Benno Watrin), and with other Anishinaabeg people through the Ojibway-Dakota Research Society. These Anishinaabemowin road markers largely emerged out of geographic knowledge spoken by generations of Anishinaabe people, then transcribed, then archived; institutionally preserved yet waiting to be brought back and breathe throughout the airspace and landscapes of Gaa-waabaabiganikaag. Of note is the advocacy work of William Madison, the White Earth Ojibwe co-founder and initial president of the Ojibway-Dakota Research Society. Madison actively sought to archive and disseminate the reports and lists generated by the society, finding ways to ensure knowledge of Ojibwe and Dakota place names would be safely stored and made publicly visible. Madison led the organization as they submitted reports to the archives of the Minnesota Historical Society,[64] unsuccessfully pushed for a booklet of Native place names to be on display at the historical society during the centennial anniversary of Minnesota statehood,[65] and was responsible for encouraging Karen Daniels Petersen to publish the society's findings – with the resulting 1963 article being a primary source relied on for the creation of the White Earth road signs.[66] Not only was Madison a literary ancestor; his and fellow Research Society members' efforts ensured that their collections of toponyms and translations would be accessible for future generations.

---

[63] Erdrich (2013, p. 18). [64] Crane (1947). [65] Madison (1957).
[66] The Ojibway-Dakota Research Society (1963, pp., 5–7).

Resonating with Erdrich's writing on name' and the spirit embedded in ancestral literary traces, the toponyms printed on the reservation road signs demonstrate the lives of Ojibwe names, movements, and presences. These markers serve as both evidence and result of Anishinaabe navigations: ancestral spatial movements between the waters of Gaa-waabaabiganikaag; forced and coerced movements through schools of linguistic elimination and cultural assimilation; movements through structures and legacies of dispossession; and, recent movements toward the expanding sonic and textual presence of Anishinaabemowin throughout the classrooms and roadways of the White Earth Reservation. White Earth author and scholar Gordon Henry describes how Gerald Vizenor undertook a project of sonic-to-textual conversion, translation, and curation of Anishinaabe dream songs into "lyric poetry" published as *Summer in the Spring*.[67] Henry theorizes what it may mean for songs to be "transpossessions," in his analysis of Frances Densmore's collecting of the songs, Vizenor's numerous publications of transcriptions with specific curatorial judgments (inclusions/additions/omissions), and the uploading of song recordings with accreditations for the singers on *Drumhop*: "In many respects, the continued regeneration of the songs, across generations, through a variety of media may tell a bigger imagi(native) story; perhaps, songs and stories cannot be contained, cannot be retained as personal, they remain transpossessive, transpossessions."[68] The presence of these public place name signs in Anishinaabemowin are articulations and manifestations of Ojibwe navigations and geographic knowledge. Henry, in noting the bond between the aforementioned dream songs/poems as palimpsests[69] and potentially transpossessions, offers insights to curatorial subjectivities[70] and enduring lives expressed through different iterations and transvaluations[71] of archived materials.

These signs in Anishinaabemowin rely on archival renderings and recordings of Ojibwe geographic knowledge and toponyms, with different iterations of place name lists, reports, and markings situated in their respective contexts and shaped by specific curatorial subjectivities. As detailed in Section 3, a principal archival document relied upon by the White Earth cultural committee when creating the signs was a 1963 *Minnesota Archaeologist* article recalled by Sonny McDougall and located by Mary Otto, which compiled earlier reports by the Ojibway-Dakota Research Society. The Research Society's reports were rooted in documenting place names spoken and shared by earlier generations of Anishinaabeg, with their descendants recording these names in the 1940s and

[67] Henry (2019, pp. 172–188). [68] Henry (2019, p. 182).
[69] Henry (2019, pp. 176–177, 179–180, 182–183). [70] Henry (2019, p. 181).
[71] Henry (2019, pp. 176–177, 179).

1950s. These archives of place names may be considered living due to their enduring influence beyond the times of their creation. Historic efforts to preserve Ojibwe place names have been critical to their present-day public presence throughout Gaa-waabaabiganikaag. Regardless of if we characterize these toponyms as "transpossessions," these place names, just like the Anishinaabe language, are alive.

2 "A Lot of It Wasn't around in the Atmosphere": Addressing Legacies of Imposed Language and Land Loss through Environmental Print in Anishinaabemowin

The place name signs for many lakes and a river throughout the White Earth Reservation are supported by the grounds of the land of white clay; a place abundant with Ojibwe life and, increasingly, language. However, the use of Anishinaabemowin by generations of White Earth citizens was suppressed by US government and Christian educational institutions that sought to assimilate Indigenous youth, disciplining them into solely speaking English. Brenda Child describes how these institutions prohibited communicating in one's own language: "All government boarding schools followed a strict policy that forbade Indian students from speaking tribal languages, the languages of their mothers and fathers."[72] Addressing the consequences of these schools on the use of Indigenous languages, Child asserts: "Former boarding school students remember being dealt with harshly for infractions of this rule. Beatings, sways from rulers, having one's mouth washed with soap or lye, or being locked in the school jail were not uncommon punishments."[73] Despite the public voicing of one's inherited language being associated with physical and psychological punishment in these settings, Indigenous youth would sometimes continue speaking the tongues of their parents and grandparents in spaces away from their instructors or other disciplinarians: "When students were threatened with discipline, tribal languages had to be spoken covertly, and they became English speakers at school. Students themselves did not necessarily abandon tribal languages in private ... Government school education, both on- and off-reservation, bears a large responsibility for the decline of Ojibwe and other tribal languages."[74]

Stories of youth being physically and psychologically reprimanded for speaking Ojibwe at assimilatory schools are documented in Vance Vannote's collection of interviews with Anishinaabekweg, *Women of White Earth* (1999). Saraphine Martin of Ponsford shared her experience attending an Indian boarding school far from Gaa-waabaabiganikaag:

> I attended the government school at Hayward, Wisconsin, for three years, starting there when I was just seven or eight years old. One day I was sitting by a lake on a hillside, talking to my friend. We were talking in our native language, and someone must have heard us. We got a strapping when we got back to the school. I had wanted to go to this school because I had a cousin who was going there, so my mother signed me up for a three-year term. After three years at this school, I couldn't understand my mother speaking Indian

[72] Child (1998, p. 40). [73] Child (1998, p. 40). [74] Child (1998, p. 40).

> when I got home, even though I could still speak a little. My grandfather also spoke the language, and I spent a lot of time with his family. He told us many stories about what happened a long time ago. It was interesting to me, and it helped me get some of my language back.[75]

In the same volume, Bonnie Faye Wadena described how her parents' generation experienced the loss of the Ojibwe language: "I have a suspicion that my mother and her generation turned against the Indian heritage during the years of the mission schools. I know they quit using the language and were discouraged from practicing any Native American traditions."[76] Irene Auginaush-Turney recalled her parents' and grandparents' experiences at Indian boarding schools: "I regret that I never learned the language. My father speaks fluently, but I don't understand it. My parents and grandparents all went to Indian boarding schools, where they were discouraged, even punished, if they used the language."[77] Myrna Joyce Smith also detailed how institutions designed to assimilate Native youth prohibited her relatives from freely speaking Ojibwe: "My grandparents spoke Ojibwe . . . and my mother was raised with it; but in school they didn't let them speak their language."[78] Ellen (Ellie Mae) Robinson articulated the relationship between American schooling and its enduring negative impacts on Anishinaabemowin fluency: "[My old mother-in-law] tried to teach me how to speak Ojibwe, but I never really learned. I think that unless you have someone to practice with, you will never become proficient. I would like to speak the language, but I didn't have enough background because we were discouraged from using it in school."[79] Joan Staples contemplated the lasting effects attending an Indian boarding school had on her father:

> I wonder what it would do to a child like my father to be taken away from his family and sent to a boarding school for three, eight, twelve years . . . The children were no longer able to speak their language, eat their traditional foods, pray in their native way, or see their families. Where were the role models to learn how to be brother, sister, husband, father, mother?[80]

Generations of White Earth Ojibwe personally felt and feel the consequences of these structural efforts to eliminate the language of the Anishinaabeg from those youth who would have otherwise gone on to teach their children and their children's children how to communicate in Ojibwe.

The aforementioned recollections of the impacts of these schools on the speech and linguistic knowledge of White Earth Ojibwe people demonstrate the connection between attending these institutions and the resulting Ojibwe

[75] Vannote and Pratt (1999, p. 74).
[76] Vannote and Pratt (1999, p. 128).
[77] Vannote and Pratt (1999, p. 144).
[78] Vannote and Pratt (1999, p. 176).
[79] Vannote and Pratt (1999, p. 190).
[80] Vannote and Pratt (1999, p. 149).

language loss for generations of Anishinaabeg. Melissa Meyer details the abundant historic presences of such institutions within the boundaries of the White Earth Reservation, on the same soils that now support these signs in the Ojibwe language. She describes how four boarding schools – the majority having affiliations with religious organizations – were created in 1890 throughout the reservation. Between the mid 1890s and early 1900s, day schools were opened in in Naytahwaush (Twin Lakes), White Earth Village, Porterville, and Pembina that focused on educating local Anishinaabe youth. Meyer notes that White Earth youth also attended boarding schools outside of Gaa-waabaabiganikaag, including "Flandreau in South Dakota," "St. John's in St. Cloud, Minnesota," "Carlisle," and "Hampton."[81] Resonating with Child's description of these schools, Meyer summarizes how these places of instruction were foundationally premised on disconnecting the children of Ojibwe parents and grandparents from their culture, their language, their identity, and their community: "Besides the trial of leaving their close-knit family group for the first time, Anishinaabe children encountered an all-out cultural assault. Teachers forbade the children to speak their native language, forcing them to converse only in English. Authorities cut the boys' hair and assigned English names to be used in place of Indian ones."[82]

The operation of these assimilatory institutions sometimes interfered in the intergenerational transmission of environmental knowledges associated with the Ojibwe seasonal round, an economy of sustainable harvests and migrations that revolved around the life rhythms and emergences of other-than-human relatives of the Anishinaabeg. The movements, migrations, and temporalities of the seasonal round were often at odds with the intentions and schedules of boarding, mission, and day schools. Members of the White Earth Reservation Curriculum Committee discuss how children would learn and assist in maple sugaring in the spring, build canoes during this season, gather berries with their mothers in the summer, and process manoomin (i.e., wild rice) in the fall.[83] These brief references to knowledge transmission to youth through harvests demonstrate how seasonal activities were – and often remain – sites of place-based education, wherein youth learn(ed) how to be in respectful relation with other-than-humans. In their 1989 history, the curriculum committee also details how Ojibwe youth learned stories about their other-than-human relatives from Elders during the winter, being taught critical lessons communicated in and interpreted from these stories.[84]

[81] Meyer (1999, p. 114). [82] Meyer (1999, p. 115).
[83] White Earth Reservation Curriculum Committee et al. (1989, pp. 13–18).
[84] White Earth Reservation Curriculum Committee et al. (1989, pp. 17–18).

The frequent incompatibility of Ojibwe youth's participation in seasonal harvests with their communities and their attendance in assimilatory schools was observed by instructors and navigated by Anishinaabe parents. Meyer details how the superintendent and a "female industrial teacher" of the Wild Rice River School in Beaulieu noted that maple sugaring and blueberry harvesting resulted in student absences. Relatedly, the manoomin harvest in the fall "often prevented children of conservative parents from securing places," further demonstrating how parents sought to have their children participate in seasonal harvests and learn associated environmental knowledge, despite these schools' desire to have Ojibwe youth in attendance. The academic calendars did not match the rhythm of the seasons and other-than-human lifecycles, with Meyer's noting that sugaring delayed returns to these schools in the spring, with ricing similarly delaying returns in the fall.[85]

The consequences of assimilatory government and religious schools interrupting seasonal harvests were not restricted to the Anishinaabeg of Gaawaabaabiganikaag. Eric Redix describes a similar dynamic in relation to the Hayward Indian School. He writes that the school was "built specifically to keep Lac Courte Oreilles children in school instead of out with their families gathering maple sugar, fishing, harvesting wild rice, and hunting. At the same time the Ojibwe struggled to continue these activities off-reservation, the murder of Joe White showed how far the state of Wisconsin was willing to go to enforce its laws."[86] The creation and growing imposition of state game laws that threatened to restrict Ojibwe seasonal harvests throughout the Great Lakes region – in violation of on- and off-reservation treaty rights[87] – temporally overlapped with these schools obstructing youth's participation in hunting, fishing, ricing, sugaring, and gathering.[88]

Returning to White Earth, Meyer further expands on the consequences of these schools in disrupting family networks and collective seasonal migrations, thereby interrupting the transmission of harvesting and environmental knowledge across generations. Meyer writes, "In the early 1890s, some parents from the eastern forests did 'all they [could] to keep their children away' from the boarding schools and took 'great satisfaction' in hiding those who ran away. Long absences from the family, sometimes amounting to years, disrupted the seasonal round, when children were a 'great help to their parents'."[89] Meyer presents the story of WayQuah (John Rogers), a White Earth Ojibwe youth who had attended boarding school for six years. Upon his and his siblings return, "their mother set about to them how to 'set rabbit snares and deadfalls' and how

[85] Meyer (1999, p. 77). [86] Redix (2014, p. 205). [87] Stark and Stark (2018, pp. 17–26).
[88] Norrgard (2014, pp. 54–56). [89] Meyer (1999, p. 116).

to set traps for larger game ... [while] insist[ing] that they use only their Anishinaabe names."[90] In addition to these schools interfering with White Earth youth's participation in seasonal activities, Meyer notes that these places of instruction required training and the undertaking of chores in government-encouraged agricultural and livestock farming.[91]

Beginning in the mid to late 1800s, these schools instructed Ojibwe girls and women in domestic labor, sewing, nursing, and education, while Ojibwe boys and men were trained in manual labor, agriculture, gardening, and livestock farming.[92] Child notes that the temporalities, rhythms, and disciplining logics of these schools were expressed in rigid schedules and restrictions of movement that infringed on the social growth of Ojibwe girls and women.[93] These schools inculcated a colonial gender binary and associated gender roles for Ojibwe youth, as addressed in the research of Kai Pyle.[94] Residential, mission, and day schools represented and enforced departures from Anishinaabe lifeways, environmental knowledge, place-based connections, and language; however, certain Ojibwe families sought to ensure the continuation of seasonal harvests and associated migrations.

We can deduce that in addition to being a "great help" during harvesting activities, White Earth youth's participation in the seasonal round was – and remains – critical for the transmission of environmental knowledge, the building of place-based relationships, the teaching of sustainable harvesting protocols, and the sharing of Anishinaabe stories and place names. The scholarship of Lawrence Gross addresses the centrality of stories and environmental experiences for building "heartstrings" to the waters, lands, and other-than-humans throughout Anishinaabe aki.[95] Gross states that there is an "interplay" between hearing Anishinaabe stories featuring other-than-human relatives and having land-based experiences bring these stories to life, together building affective connections to place for Ojibwe youth.[96] Gross's research helps contextualize the efforts of White Earth Ojibwe parents to have their children remain involved in seasonal harvests despite obstacles posed by mission, day, and boarding schools.

Forms of Indigenous resistance and Ojibwe survivance were also present on and near the grounds of these schools. In addition to students clandestinely speaking Anishinaabemowin in private while attending these institutions, parents also migrated to areas surrounding these schools at White Earth. Meyer describes how boarding schools on the White Earth Reservation influenced where Ojibwe families decided to reside: "Instead of establishing homesteads

[90] Meyer (1999, p. 117). [91] Meyer (1999, p. 115). [92] Meyer (1999, pp. 114–115, 214).
[93] Child (2012, pp. 132–133). [94] Pyle (2020, pp. 110–113).
[95] Gross (2014, pp. 155–157, 164–165). [96] Gross (2014, pp. 157, 160).

on their allotments, most conservative Indians . . . [lived] in areas convenient to meet their economic and social needs without regard to 'legal' ownership. Boarding schools located at Pine Point, Wild Rice River, and White Earth Village served as focal points for settlements of families that relocated to be closer to their children."[97] Despite these parents' dedicated efforts to retain familial connections, the speaking of the Ojibwe language would become less and less common due to these institutions and their legacies. The Anishinaabemowin fluency rate of the White Earth Ojibwe is currently at levels that threaten the future existence of the language. This is reflected in a March 2022 message about a new Ojibwe language immersion program from White Earth Chairman Michael Fairbanks, which appeared in *Anishinaabeg Today*: "Our Gaa-waabaabiganikaag Nation has less than 50 fluent speakers across the 17,500 + band membership. So it is vital to keep our language alive."[98]

This Element investigates how the bilingual place name signs – in their origin, installation, and observation – create space for Anishinaabemowin and Ojibwe geographic knowledge to be publicly witnessed, for a community and reservation that's still grappling with the lasting consequences of settler state-facilitated projects of assimilation via the "education" of Indigenous youth. In this Element, I investigate how historic efforts to preserve Ojibwe place names have informed the revitalization of these designations for bodies of water throughout the White Earth Reservation. Further, I draw on ethnographic evidence to trace how the recent emergence of these names on public road signs informs White Earth Ojibwe senses of place and belonging on Gaa-waabaabiganikaag. I argue that despite the White Earth Reservation currently being home to a limited number of Anishinaabemowin speakers, these signs mark Gaa-waabaabiganikaag with Ojibwe presence while reflecting visions of linguistic futures and growing fluencies.

Origins of the Signs, Overview of the Project

The signs in Anishinaabemowin were installed in 2016, emerging through the efforts of the White Earth Nation's Education and Cultural Divisions, with assistance from the WEN's Division of Public Works and the Minnesota Department of Transportation for installation.[99] Drawing on ethnographic interviews with Mary Otto (White Earth Ojibwe), the former WEN Director of Education, and Merlin (White Earth Ojibwe/Dakota), the Director of the nation's Cultural Division, I tell the story of how these Anishinaabemowin road

[97] Meyer (1991, p. 390). [98] *Anishinaabeg Today* (2022, p. 9).
[99] *Anishinaabeg Today* (2016, p. 1).

Figure 3 Asaawe Zaaga'igan sign. Photo by author.

signs were conceived and realized. As described next, both Mary and Merlin were motivated to create these signs due to their commitment to make Ojibwe place names visible within the boundaries of the reservation (see Figure 3). Through the efforts of White Earth personnel, the signs were funded by a grant from the Minnesota Indian Affairs Council via a "legislative appropriation to preserve the arts and cultural heritage of Minnesota."[100] Initially, the signs could only be seen when traveling one direction. However, as Merlin told me, the White Earth Nation decided to fund an additional set of signs so that the Anishinaabemowin place names are visible when traveling both ways on the roads next to where they are posted.[101]

During a July 2021 interview, Mary shared how she imagined the concept behind the signs while working as an educator with Ojibwe youth and hearing about a similar project on another Ojibwe reservation. On the inspiration for the signs, she stated: "I had seen a newspaper article where Fond du Lac [Band of Lake Superior Chippewa] had done some road signs, and I was like, 'Why don't we have anything like that?'" Emphasizing the need for Ojibwe environmental print throughout the reservation, she described how the construction of these signs was intended to demonstrate the vitality and endurance of the language in the lived world, external to the classrooms where Ojibwe youth are becoming

[100] *Anishinaabeg Today* (2016, p. 1).
[101] "Interview with Merlin [Last Name Redacted]," interview conducted by Elan Pochedley, White Earth Reservation, August 2, 2017.

speakers of Anishinaabemowin. When I asked Mary how she understood the relationship between Ojibwe language revitalization and the installation of the road signs, she responded:

> So being a teacher and trying to incorporate Ojibwe language in the classroom . . . And learning that our students have environmental print all around them; whether its Cheerios, like if they see a Cheerios box, or pull into a Walmart parking lot, or go by a McDonald's sign, our kids – as soon as they're verbal – they can make that connection. So doing the signs was one way, I felt, [for] reclaiming and stating to our children that our language is alive, it's still alive, and it's a living thing, and that it should be all around us – especially on our own lands – [for when] our children are traveling in cars or in buses with their parents – and all of our Band members, not just their children.[102]

She described how this project emerged in the context of low language fluency among White Earth families: "I feel that language has been taken from us, and not by any fault of our own. But it used to be, just like with the English language, you learn it at home from your parents, your siblings, your caregivers."[103] Similar sentiments were conveyed to me in other interviews conducted between 2017 and 2021 with White Earth citizens and descendants.

The emphasis on making these signs visible on public roads stands in contrast to the relegation of speaking Anishinaabemowin to private spaces for Ojibwe children who attended boarding, mission, and day schools, wherein their original language was forbidden by educators. While these schools were historically sites of language suppression and loss, today's Ojibwe youth of the White Earth Nation are learning Anishinaabemowin in their classrooms on Gaawaabaabiganikaag. While many of their parents and grandparents did not have accessible options for learning the language growing up, Mary described how the children of the reservation are becoming the educators of Anishinaabemowin within their families: "And with the Ojibwe language being in the crisis that it is, we now are seeing that our children are probably gonna be the ones teaching the language in the home and giving the language back. They have more opportunities through immersion school or childcare settings where the language is given more of an opportunity."[104] In the summer of 2017, Monica Hedstrom (White Earth Ojibwe), then WEN Director of Natural Resources, shared a similar observation on how young Ojibwe of the reservation are increasingly being taught the language in Head Start programs: "They had language at Head Start. U of M [University of Minnesota] would come up, putting together some curriculum for it. They're learning it more and

[102] "Interview with Mary Otto," interview virtually conducted by Elan Pochedley, July 22, 2021.
[103] "Interview with Mary Otto," interview virtually conducted by Elan Pochedley, July 22, 2021.
[104] "Interview with Mary Otto," interview virtually conducted by Elan Pochedley, July 22, 2021.

more in those schools. Gosh, those kids are lucky."[105] In July 2017, Megan Bakken (White Earth Ojibwe), who is now the Manager of the WEN Land Office, described how her children were gaining knowledge of the language through the local Head Start, preserving it for themselves and future generations: "But now the kids have the option of learning Ojibwe. And they learn it from Head Start. So [with] all my little kids, I'm actually learning little bits. I can count to five, but that's about it. But with them learning it too, it should help preserve it."[106] Will Bement (White Earth Ojibwe), the WEN Fisheries Manager, shared a similar experience of learning Anishinaabemowin from his children, who have become familiar with the Ojibwe language through immersive educational experiences: "I have a kindergartener and a second grader. My kids will come home and just rattle off whole sentences and they'll go, 'Dad, you don't know what I'm talking about?' 'No, I don't!' [*Laughter*] But no, they're implementing that in the schools too, which is good. My kids vastly know more than me on this stuff."[107] Mary summed up the shifting generational roles of Ojibwe language education when she told me, "It's often, and I think now, the pendulum has changed where our children are gonna be the ones that are bringing the language back to the center of our homes."[108]

Mary's stated motivation behind the signage project was to visually ensure that White Earth youth and citizens understand that their "language is alive, it's still alive, and it's a living thing, and that it should be all around us – especially on our own lands." The signs, in conjunction with language classes offered through White Earth schools and Head Start programs, create an environment wherein Anishinaabemowin is encountered regularly by Tribal youth and their families. Katherine Warren (Mississippi Band of Anishinaabe and White Earth Descendant), the former manager of the WEN Land Office, described how the language's presence at Gaa-waabaabiganikaag had largely vanished as a result of the assimilatory focus of previous government- and mission-operated schools:

> When the mission schools came through their purpose was to remove the identity and break down family associations which were taught through language. The act of using your customs and language was strictly prohibited, resulting in family connections being lost and not knowing how to communicate effectively anymore. Life lessons, expressions, and how to make

[105] "Interview with Monica Hedstrom," interview conducted by Elan Pochedley, White Earth Reservation, July 17, 2017.

[106] "Interview with Megan Bakken," interview conducted by Elan Pochedley, White Earth Reservation, July 20, 2017.

[107] "Interview with Will Bement," interview conducted by Elan Pochedley, White Earth Reservation, August 3, 2017.

[108] "Interview with Mary Otto," interview virtually conducted by Elan Pochedley, July 22, 2021.

> decisions were taught through our oral language. We saw a lot of disconnection, and the language was not passed on. Unless you were learning from your family it just was not around in our surrounding atmosphere. It has progressed to cause a lot of dysfunction and dependency problems today. It is sad that our language is not strong and prevalent. I feel I missed out on a lot of teaching and understanding. Not only of my heritage but to pass it on to future generations. I know words but speaking fluently and interpreting when spoken is very difficult.[109]

Mary highlighted how immersing White Earth youth in the language is crucial for ensuring that they find power and support in their identity as Anishinaabe people. On the relationship between the language and the strength of Ojibwe youth, Mary shared:

> I did language revitalization work. I worked with grants. I did a lot of work with language, with my belief that language is who we are, it's not separate from culture, and thinking it would give our students more of their identity of them as Anishinaabe and give 'em that inner-strength and resilience . . .[110]

The introduction of this environmental print, exposing travelers to the Ojibwe language and geographic place names, was envisioned as creating an atmosphere wherein Anishinaabemowin is not silenced, but, rather, highly visible.

[109] "Interview with Katherine Warren," interview conducted by Elan Pochedley, White Earth Reservation, July 19, 2017. Includes additions submitted on February 6, 2025.

[110] "Interview with Mary Otto," interview virtually conducted by Elan Pochedley, July 22, 2021.

3 Archival Diving and Atmosphere Building for Ojibwe Futures: Intergenerational Curation and Cultivation of Geographic Knowledge

Earlier efforts to record and preserve Ojibwe place names for aquatic bodies throughout Gaa-waabaabiganikaag and surrounding regions generated the source materials that White Earth Nation citizens and personnel would rely on for the signage project. In January 1963, Karen Daniels Petersen, Research Assistant in Ethnology of the Science Museum of St. Paul, published a list of Ojibwe and Dakota place names, English translations of their meanings, and English names of the associated locations in *The Minnesota Archaeologist.*[111] These geographic designations and associated translations were documented through the efforts of an organization known as the Ojibway-Dakota Research Society of Minnesota[112] throughout the 1940s and 1950s. In her introduction to the list, Petersen shared how she had been contacted by William Madison (White Earth Band of Ojibwe), the head of the Research Society, to publish the organization's recordings and translations of original Ojibwe toponyms of lakes, rivers, and other locations. Petersen commented on Madison's unwavering commitment to record these geographic designations and disseminate them to the public: "When meetings ceased Mr. Madison's devotion to the work never flagged. He carefully preserved all the pertinent papers and kept looking for a publisher for them. It was he who brought them to this editor's attention late in 1958 . . . He died December 9, 1959."[113] This publication would later prove to be a critical reference source for the development of the Anishinaabemowin place name signs installed roughly five decades after this issue of *The Minnesota Archaeologist* was published. In a September 2022 email communication, Mary Otto confirmed that she and Leonard "Sonny" McDougall relied on Petersen's 1963 article on place names recorded by the Ojibway-Dakota Research Society as the reference source for their Anishinaabemowin signage project. In presenting the curated list of toponyms in 1963, Petersen identifies the sole creator of this work: "The author of the present papers is truly the Ojibway-Dakota Research Society."[114]

Motivations and Methods for Preserving Ojibwe Place Names

Petersen described how the Ojibway-Dakota Research Society (initially founded as the Ojibway Research Society of Minnesota) ended up focusing

[111] Ojibway-Dakota Research Society of Minnesota (1963, pp. 5–6).

[112] Note: The society was originally known as the "Ojibway Research Society of Minnesota," as included in its first report completed on April 1, 1944.

[113] Ojibway-Dakota Research Society of Minnesota (1963, pp. 3, 5–7).

[114] Ojibway-Dakota Research Society of Minnesota (1963, p. 7).

largely on different lakes and rivers' names. After Madison had initially undertaken the project of translating the meanings of Ojibwe people's names included in an 1889 agreement, a friend brought to his attention the numerous names for bodies of water in Anishinaabemowin:

> One of the group mentioned the abundance of Ojibway names for lakes and rivers, and proposed translating them. For this purpose Mr. Madison, Archie Libby and Joseph E. Fairbanks met one evening in September, 1942. Thus the society began that was to meet intermittently until 1955 . . . The organization [voted] on November 26, 1944, to invite members of the Dakota tribe to join.[115]

The co-founders and officers of the society, William Madison and Joseph Fairbanks, were from the White Earth Reservation (see Figures 4 and 5).[116] With the Research Society meeting in Minneapolis throughout the 1940s and 1950s at the home of John L. Gleason – a non-Native member of the Minnesota Archaeological Society[117] –, these Anishinaabe researchers originally from Gaa-waabaabiganikaag were constructing an intellectual space within the Twin Cities focused on documenting Ojibwe and Dakota place names.

Figure 4 Members of the Ojibway-Dakota Research Society of Minnesota, from Ed Crane's 1947 *Minneapolis Tribune* article. Images courtesy of the Minnesota Historical Society[118]

[115] Ojibway-Dakota Research Society of Minnesota (1963, pp. 5–6).
[116] Ojibway-Dakota Research Society of Minnesota (1945, *Report No. 2*, p. 12).
[117] Ojibway-Dakota Research Society of Minnesota (1963, pp. 4, 7). [118] Crane (1947).

Figure 5 Members of the Ojibway-Dakota Research Society of Minnesota, from Ed Crane's 1947 *Minneapolis Tribune* article. Images courtesy of the Minnesota Historical Society[119]

The preservation of Ojibwe geographical knowledge by this mid twentieth-century Research Society was not an isolated attempt at recording Anishinaabe place names. Rev. Joseph Alexander Gilfillan was an Episcopal missionary based on the White Earth Reservation beginning in 1873.[120] In April 1885, Gilfillan submitted to the Minnesota Historical Society a collection of Ojibwe place names within the White Earth Reservation, throughout the state, and "in the adjoining territories of Dakota, Manitoba, and state of Wisconsin."[121] He described learning names over approximately thirteen years, along with chronicling others with the help of "Indians and mixed bloods familiar with the different localities by having journeyed or lived there."[122] Unfortunately, Gilfillan did not include the names of Ojibwe people who shared Anishinaabemowin toponyms with the missionary or elaborate on their intentions behind supporting the creation of this list.

In his introductory remarks to the 1885 list of Ojibwe place names, Gilfillan framed his work's significance in relation to the geographic knowledge of Ojibwe people, their presences surrounding Anishinaabe homewaters, and an implicit expectation of their disappearance related to the imminent settlement of Euro-Americans within Anishinaabe aki. The missionary's rationales and assumptions underlying this project reflect what

[119] Crane (1947). [120] "Anthropologic Miscellanea" (1913, pp. 712–713).
[121] Gilfillan (1885, pp. 451–477). [122] Gilfillan (1885, p. 452).

Jean O'Brien refers to as the "lasting" of Indigenous peoples, wherein local non-Native historians have employed a rhetorical strategy that casts Native peoples as outside of modernity and Euro-Americans as within the (then) contemporary present. Such writers craft stories of Euro-American belonging through strategic narrations of Indigenous disappearance.[123] Noting that Gilfillan's list of place names was conceived of as a gift "to science and those who shall come after us," the missionary articulated how he imagined the significance of *historic* Ojibwe place names for *future* Euro-American occupants of Anishinaabe aki: "They will be interested in knowing what the first inhabitants named the places where they will have reared their happy homes and often an interest beyond that of mere curiosity will attach to those names."[124] Further, Gilfillan suggested that Euro-Americans' fascination with the names would be correlated with their settlement of Ojibwe territory, writing, "Many of the names are in localities yet unsettled by white men, but they will be settled one day, and in the near future, and then those names will be of interest."[125]

Those who documented historic place names of the Ojibwe have held conflicting perspectives on the endurance or erasure of Indigenous toponyms following Euro-American settlement. In Gilfillan's 1885 introduction, he described how original or earlier names endure, despite the dislocation of the peoples who created or witnessed these identifiers of place: "Names cling very tenaciously and survive the total sweeping away of the ancient inhabitants who named them; as is abundantly evidenced in our own country and in those beyond the sea, where the names of localities given by the original Irish race, for instance, remain, though another race totally different in blood, religion and language has come in and occupied their place."[126]

Here, the reverend – raised in Ireland and of Scotch-Irish descent[127] – claimed names endure the "sweeping away of the ancient inhabitants," with Gilfillan's work itself being premised on preserving these names for future white Americans expected to soon reside on the soils and navigate the homewaters of the Ojibwe. In contrast, a 1947 article by Ed Crane, a staff writer of the *Minneapolis Tribune*, referenced how members of the Ojibway-Dakota Research Society conveyed the toponymic consequences of their peoples' and nations' dispossession: "STOLEN PROPERTY So declare members of the Ojibway-Dakota Research Society of Minnesota . . . The Indians prove their charge by pointing to the names the whites have tacked onto the land they stole from America's aborigines."[128] Here, Research Society members nuanced how

[123] O'Brien (2010, pp. xii, 107). [124] Gilfillan (1885, p. 451). [125] Gilfillan (1885, p. 452).
[126] Gilfillan (1885, p. 452). [127] "Anthropologic Miscellanea" (1913, pp. 712–713).
[128] Crane (1947).

the Minneapolis public should understand settler state praxes and legacies of claiming and naming. With Gilfillan attesting in the 1880s that Native place names would endure despite the displacement of Indigenous peoples, and with the Research Society asserting in the 1940s that Anishinaabe designations had been replaced by English toponyms, it's striking that these chroniclers and curators with starkly different understandings participated in similar acts of recording Ojibwe names of waters. Despite such conflicting ideas, these preservationists agreed that Anishinaabe geographic designations and their meanings should be documented and shared with the public. This is evidenced in Gilfillan and the Ojibway-Dakota Research Society submitting their respective reports to the Minnesota Historical Society.[129]

So what were the motivations and goals of the Ojibway-Dakota Research Society that guided Ojibwe members' efforts to document their people's place names? I argue, based on the methods adopted by the Research Society and the extant records of the organization housed at the Minnesota Historical Society, members of this group were invested in delving deep into the rich meanings embedded within the Ojibwe language. This is reflected in co-founder William Madison's summary of the society's purpose. In a 1957 letter to Russell Fridley, the director of the Minnesota Historical Society, Madison described the organization's focus:

> The purpose and object of the Society is to obtain and record such information . . . revealing the history and culture of the original people of the state. The Society believes that while it's [*sic*] membership has a wide command of the Ojibway-Dakota tongues, it's [*sic*] knowledge may not be complete, and it welcomes information from any source which will contribute to accuracy and coverage in it's [*sic*] reports.[130]

In "revealing" this "history and culture," this sentiment refers to the society's close examination of geographic designations passed on across generations to understand and translate their meanings.

My interpretation of this excerpt is rooted less in the polished reports of the Research Society, being more so derived from the archived prints and pencil strokes appearing in seemingly unfinished reports. Petersen noted how works-in -progress were discovered in the personal collection of John Gleason: " . . . three additional incomplete reports were found in his papers . . . fragmentary, repetitions of material in earlier reports, and for the most part compiled from such published sources as Nicollet, Gilfillan and Williamson."[131] In the 1957 letter to Fridley, Madison articulated the Research Society's intentions when engaging

[129] Minnesota Historical Society (1944, p. 304); and, Minnesota Historical Society (1947, p. 374).
[130] Madison (1957). [131] Ojibway-Dakota Research Society of Minnesota (1963, p. 7).

with previous records of Ojibwe geographic designations: "It is not the purpose of the Society to criti[ic]ize the works of any writer in using the languages, but we are interested in the usages of Indian words to secure a more exact meaning and therefore; our suggestions will be found in Rev. Gilfillan's and Capt. Pope ['s] works in naming lakes and streams in Minnesota."[132] Premised on understanding the meanings encased within the Anishinaabemowin toponyms for bodies of water, reports featuring graphite and ink marks – deviating from the typeface – demonstrate how the Anishinaabemowin speakers of the Research Society engaged with previously documented versions of place names. Pictured next are examples of the inscribed remnants of the group's examination, reflection, and interpretation of names previously archived by Gilfillan (1885) and mapped by Joseph Nicolas Nicollet (1843) (see Figures 6 and 7).

The Ojibway-Dakota Research Society's meetings throughout the 1940s and 1950s occurred during a period of increasing Ojibwe migrations to the Twin Cities. Nancy Shoemaker notes how Ojibwe and Dakota migrations during the

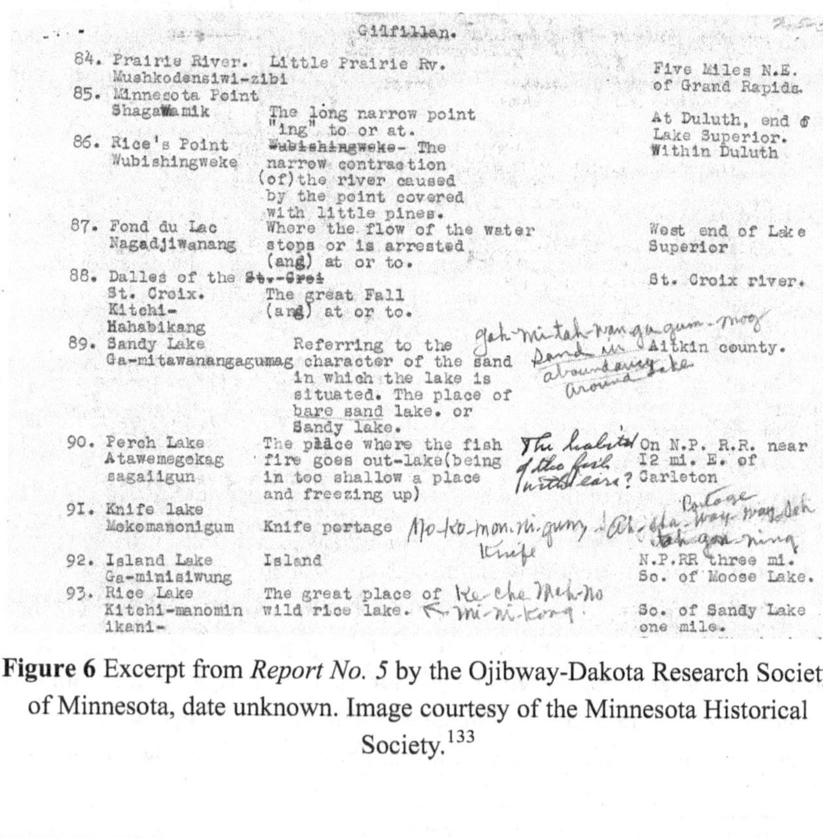

Gilfillan.

84. Prairie River. Mushkodensiwi-zibi	Little Prairie Rv.	Five Miles N.E. of Grand Rapids.
85. Minnesota Point Shagawamik	The long narrow point "ing" to or at.	At Duluth, end of Lake Superior.
86. Rice's Point Wubishingweke	Wubishingweke- The narrow contraction (of) the river caused by the point covered with little pines.	Within Duluth
87. Fond du Lac Nagadjiwanang	Where the flow of the water stops or is arrested (ang) at or to.	West end of Lake Superior
88. Dalles of the St. Croix. Kitchi-Kahabikang	The great Fall (ang) at or to.	St. Croix river.
89. Sandy Lake Ga-mitawanangagumag	Referring to the character of the sand in which the lake is situated. The place of bare sand lake. or Sandy lake.	Aitkin county.
90. Perch Lake Atawemegokag sagaiigun	The place where the fish fire goes out-lake(being in too shallow a place and freezing up)	On N.P. R.R. near I2 mi. E. of Carleton
9I. Knife lake Mokomanonigum	Knife portage	
92. Island Lake Ga-minisiwung	Island	N.P.RR three mi. So. of Moose Lake.
93. Rice Lake Kitchi-manomin ikani-	The great place of wild rice lake.	So. of Sandy Lake one mile.

Figure 6 Excerpt from *Report No. 5* by the Ojibway-Dakota Research Society of Minnesota, date unknown. Image courtesy of the Minnesota Historical Society.[133]

[132] Madison (1957). [133] Ojibway-Dakota Research Society of Minnesota (n.d., *Report No. 5*).

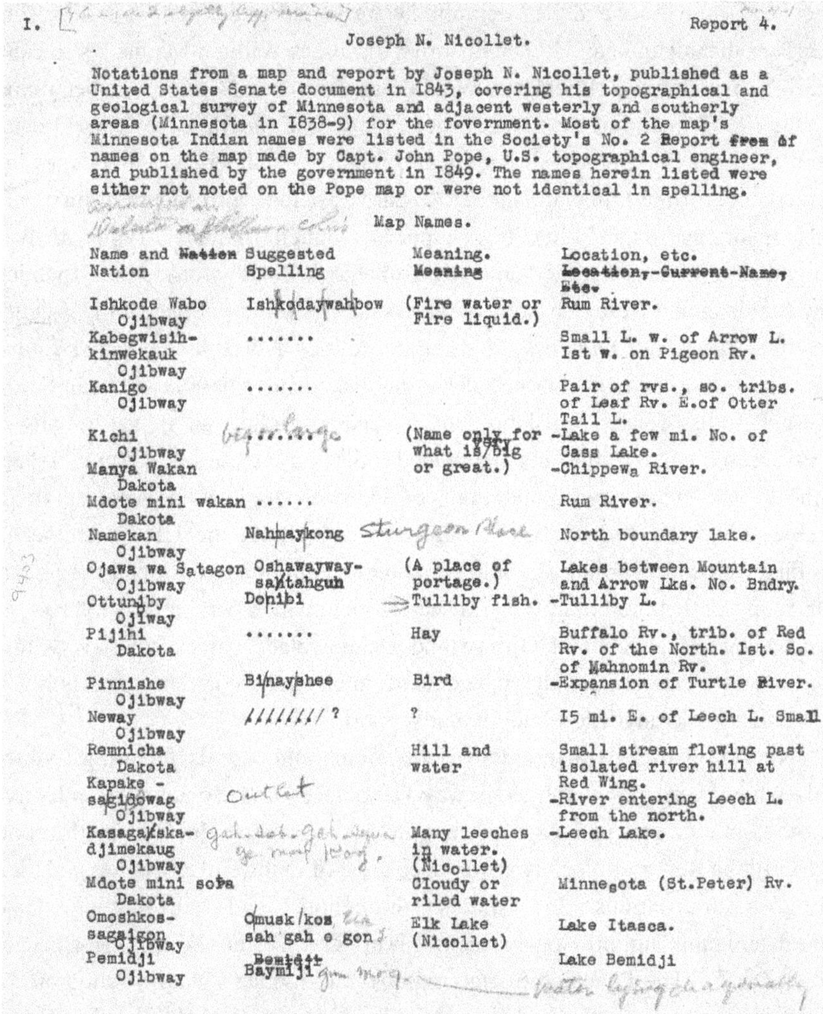

I. Report 4.

Joseph N. Nicollet.

Notations from a map and report by Joseph N. Nicollet, published as a United States Senate document in 1843, covering his topographical and geological survey of Minnesota and adjacent westerly and southerly areas (Minnesota in 1838-9) for the fovernment. Most of the map's Minnesota Indian names were listed in the Society's No. 2 Report of names on the map made by Capt. John Pope, U.S. topographical engineer, and published by the government in 1849. The names herein listed were either not noted on the Pope map or were not identical in spelling.

Map Names.

Name and Nation	Suggested Spelling	Meaning.	Location, etc.
Ishkode Wabo Ojibway	Ishkodaywahbow	(Fire water or Fire liquid.)	Rum River.
Kabegwisih-kinwekauk Ojibway	....		Small L. w. of Arrow L. Ist w. on Pigeon Rv.
Kanigo Ojibway	....		Pair of rvs., so. tribs. of Leaf Rv. E.of Otter Tail L.
Kichi Ojibway	....	(Name only for what is very big or great.)	-Lake a few mi. No. of Cass Lake.
Manya Wakan Dakota			-Chippewa River.
Mdote mini wakan Dakota	......		Rum River.
Namekan Ojibway	Nahmaykong	Sturgeon Place	North boundary lake.
Ojawa wa Satagon Ojibway	Oshawayway-sahtahguh	(A place of portage.)	Lakes between Mountain and Arrow Lks. No. Bndry.
Ottunibby Ojiway	Donibi	Tulliby fish.	-Tulliby L.
Pijihi Dakota	....	Hay	Buffalo Rv., trib. of Red Rv. of the North. Ist. So. of Mahnomin Rv.
Pinnishe Ojibway	Binayshee	Bird	-Expansion of Turtle River.
Neway Ojibway	///////// ?	?	I5 mi. E. of Leech L. Small
Remnicha Dakota		Hill and water	Small stream flowing past isolated river hill at Red Wing.
Kapake - sagidowag Ojibway	Outlet		-River entering Leech L. from the north.
Kasagaska-djimekaug Ojibway		Many leeches in water. (Nicollet)	-Leech Lake.
Mdote mini sota Dakota		Cloudy or riled water	Minnesota (St.Peter) Rv.
Omoshkos-sagaigon Ojibway	Omusk/kos sah gah e gon	Elk Lake (Nicollet)	Lake Itasca.
Pemidji Ojibway	Baymiji		Lake Bemidji

Figure 7 Excerpt from *Report No. 4* by the Ojibway-Dakota Research Society of Minnesota, date unknown. Image courtesy of the Minnesota Historical Society.[134]

early to mid twentieth century allowed for them “to become allies,” with Native peoples’ journeys to Minneapolis and Saint Paul surrounding World War II being a result of “plentiful jobs and high paying defense work [that] attracted Indians to the Twin Cities.”[135] Shoemaker notes that Anishinaabe people with roots at White Earth were most strongly represented among the Indigenous peoples of the Twin Cities during this time, demonstrating that connections

[134] Ojibway-Dakota Research Society of Minnesota (n.d., *Report No. 4*).

[135] Shoemaker (1988, pp. 432, 434).

between these cities and the reservation were shared across many families from Gaa-waabaabiganikaag.[136] The historian discusses William Madison's roles in early urban Native political and social organizations in Minneapolis beginning in the 1920s, including the "Twin Cities Chippewa Council," "the Tepee Order," and the national "Society of American Indians."[137] Shoemaker associates the emergence of the Ojibway-Dakota Research Society with founding members also belonging to the Twin Cities Chippewa Council. In the late 1940s, another organization known as the "Ojibway Tomahawk Band" would be co-founded by Madison and Research Society members. The Band published a newsletter entitled *The New Tomahawk*, focusing on politics and Ojibwe people's rights. Shoemaker notes that "the newsletter published information and opinion on current Indian-related legislation and pushed for rights guaranteed Indians as American citizens and rights guaranteed Indians by treaties."[138] Anton Treuer traces how subsequent generations of Ojibwe people who grew up in or relocated to the Twin Cities – largely as a result of the US government's Indian Relocation policy – would collaborate, continue to politically organize, and support their community.[139] Research Society members' efforts to preserve and accurately document Ojibwe and Dakota place names emerged within a context of international engagement, intellectual collaboration, political organizing and advocacy, and mutual support.

While engaging with previous publications and reports featuring Ojibwe place names, members of the Ojibway-Dakota Research Society were attentive to the sources and pathways of geographic knowledge. In their sixth report (1850), the Research Society reproduced a list of Ojibwe place names and their English translations for waters throughout and surrounding Gaa-waabaabiganikaag previously included in Rev. Benno Watrin's history of Ponsford.[140] The Research Society notes the individuals Watrin relied on for this geographic knowledge featured in *The Ponsfordian* (1930), who Watrin credited in his book's introduction:[141] "The authorities were principally J.W. Nunn, Charles [Charley] Moulton, N.B. Hurr, John Broker, and John Rabbit."[142] Watrin also relied on Warren Upham's 1920 report on Ojibwe place names.[143] In the Ojibway-Dakota Research Society's reports 2–6 housed by the Minnesota Historical Society, the names of those sharing their geographic knowledge of place names, their meanings, and/or associated stories

[136] Shoemaker (1988, pp. 437–438).
[137] Shoemaker (1988, pp. 436, 438–441).
[138] Shoemaker (1988, pp. 444–445).
[139] Treuer (2010, pp. 54, 63–65).
[140] Ojibway-Dakota Research Society of Minnesota (1950, *Report No. 6*).
[141] Watrin (1930, pp. 7–8).
[142] Ojibway-Dakota Research Society of Minnesota (1950, *Report No. 6*, pp. 3–4).
[143] Upham (1920); and, Watrin (1930, pp. 7–8).

is frequently, though not always, referenced: specific Ojibwe and Dakota "authorities" for certain toponyms and stories, names of society members contributing to respective reports, those whose previously archived lists are drawn on, and, when available, those who shared their geographic knowledge for the production of lists recorded prior to the society's own.[144]

In being attentive to the *transmission* of Ojibwe and Dakota geographic toponyms, meanings, and sometimes place-based stories, I suggest the society was practicing and textually inscribing relational forms of knowledge transference, interpretation, curation, (re)presentation, and (re)production. For example, the inclusion of informants' identities for Watrin's book in *Report 6* presents a map of names – that we can trace and research – revealing how geographic knowledge traveled between Watrin's informants, to the text of *The Ponsfordian*, and then to the Ojibway-Dakota Research Society. *John Rabbit* (*O shee gonce*) lived in Pine Point and was elected as a delegate by the White Earth Local Council to attend the "General Council of the Chippewas of Minnesota" in Bemidji in 1916 and 1920.[145] *J.W.* [*James*] *Nunn* was a trader and banker who wrote a reflection on the desecration of forests surrounding Pine Point due to the overharvesting practices of lumber companies.[146] *Charley/Charles Moulton* was "a member of the Otter Tail band of Chippewa," according to ethnologist Frances Densmore.[147] In *The Ponsfordian* (1930), Watrin includes the history of Ojibwe resistance to illegal timber harvesting by the Commonwealth Lumber Company at Round Lake in 1901. Moulton assisted in resolving this conflict, while afterward serving as an interpreter for the Ojibwe suing the Indian agent and the successor lumber company.[148] In *The Ponsfordian*, *N.B. Hurr* (*Now-ah-quay-gi-shig*) was described as "an Ottawa" from Oklahoma.[149] Hurr's writing on the implementation of the 1906 Clapp Act at White Earth would later be cited in works by Paulette Fairbanks Molin[150] and Colin Calloway.[151] Hurr served as the director of the Pine Point School on the White Earth Reservation between 1903 and 1911.[152] In April 1934, *John Broker* of Ponsford served as a delegate representing White Earth for the "Indian

144 "Society Records, 1944–1959" of the Ojibway-Dakota Research Society of Minnesota, Folders 3–8, Minnesota Historical Society, Saint Paul, MN.

145 *The Tomahawk* (June 1916, p. 1); *The Tomahawk* (December 1916, p. 8); *The Tomahawk* (1920, p. 1); and, *The Tomahawk* (1921, p. 4).

146 Watrin (1930, pp. 13–14, 16–18); Wilcox (1907, pp. 68–69); and, Molin (1983, pp. xii–xiii).

147 Densmore (1910, pp. 79–80).

148 Watrin (1930, pp. 45–46); and, U.S. Congress (1912). Note: See Watrin's history reprinted in Gudmundson (2018).

149 Watrin (1930, p. 43).

150 Molin (1983, pp. xi–xii); and, University of Minnesota Morris (n.d.).

151 Calloway (2004, pp. 342, 363).

152 Watrin (1930, pp. 34, 43–44); Wierima (2011); and, *The Tomahawk* (1903, p. 4).

Congress" held in Hayward, Wisconsin, concerning the Indian Reorganization Act (IRA).[153] Broker would later become the first president of the Minnesota Chippewa Tribe's Tribal Executive Committee (TEC) in 1936, following the restructuring of Ojibwe governance structures under the IRA.[154]

In recording not only Ojibwe toponyms and their translations but also the names of those who shared this geographic knowledge, the Ojibway-Dakota Research Society presented genealogical maps of the movements of knowledge concerning Ojibwe place names. In drawing on both Society members' own geographic knowledge and previously recorded lists of Anishinaabemowin toponyms, the Research Society's reports would serve as the most critical archive for the creation of road signs now found throughout Gaa-waabaabiganikaag (see Figure 8).

Collaborative and Cooperative Naming

The approach taken by the White Earth Nation's cultural committee for determining names and locations for Ojibwe language signs resonates with the Ojibway-Dakota Research Society's collaborative process for collectively evaluating and agreeing on spellings and translations of Anishinaabemowin toponyms in the mid twentieth century. Petersen summarized the Research Society's dialogic method for determining the spellings and meanings of names: "The procedure at meetings was informal. A member brought up for consideration a place name found on a map, or perhaps one handed down to him by his forebears. All members were free to suggest the proper Indian form and meaning. When an agreement was reached the conclusions were recorded by the secretary."[155] With the organization co-founded by Ojibwe folks from White Earth – Madison and Fairbanks – *what can we learn by analyzing and comparing these processes of publicly recording and inscribing designations for place across generations of Anishinaabeg from Gaa-waabaabiganikaag?*

During a 2017 interview, Merlin described the committee that initiated the signage project by applying for a grant:

> The Tribe about five years ago started a TLC – Tradition, Language, Culture – Committee. So it was comprised of certain divisions, divisional directors, and they would meet ... There was five or six people on that committee ... The Educational Director was Joan LaVoy and Mary Otto was the Assistant Director ... So they wrote a grant ... [and] got the grant to start the Ojibwemowin signs.[156]

[153] Wilkins (2019, pp. 21–22).

[154] Minnesota Chippewa Tribe (1936, p. 4); and, Schaaf and Robertson (1978, p. 107).

[155] Ojibway-Dakota Research Society of Minnesota (1963, p. 6).

[156] "Interview with Merlin," interview conducted by Elan Pochedley, White Earth Reservation, August 2, 2017.

MEMBERSHIP LIST

Mr. and Mrs. William Anywaush, Ojibway
William Aspinwall, Ojibway
Mrs. Susan Bahr, Dakota
Edward Beaulieu, Ojibway
Paul Beaulieu, Ojibway
Niles Beaupre, Ojibway
David Belland, Ojibway
Mrs. Ellen M. Bellanger, Ojibway
Mr. and Mrs. Edward W. Carl, Ojibway
William Chatfield, Ojibway
Charlie Daydodge, Ojibway
Mrs. Mary Doehle, Ojibway
Mrs. Romona Erickson, Dakota
Joseph E. Fairbanks, Ojibway
Mr. and Mrs. George Garvie, Dakota & Ojibway
Mrs. Bessie James, Dakota
John Jekey, Ojibway
Anna Johnson, Ojibway
Mrs. Louise Knight, Ojibway
Mr. and Mrs. Paul LaRoque, Ojibway
Mr. and Mrs. Harry Lawrence, Dakota
Archie Libby, Ojibway
Mr. and Mrs. William Little Wolf, Ojibway
Mr. and Mrs. James Longie, Cree
Paul Lufkins, Ojibway
James McIntosh, Ojibway
William Madison, Ojibway
Mr. and Mrs. Richard Manypenny, Ojibway
Mrs. Agnes Miller, Dakota
Mrs. Louise Peake, Ojibway
John Pell, Ojibway
William Pell, Ojibway
Mrs. Angeline Rice, Ojibway
Mrs. Cora Rice, Iroquois
Mrs. Jane Robertson, Dakota
Mrs. Elizabeth Rock, Oneida
Mr. and Mrs. James Roy, Ojibway
George Selkirk, Ojibway
Henry Selkirk, Ojibway
Mrs. Elizabeth Sheppard, Ojibway
Farn Sheppard, Ojibway
Peter Sitting, Ojibway
Richard Smith, Ojibway
Alex J. Whitefeather, Ojibway

Localities represented:

Minnesota - Cass Lake, Grand Portage, Leech Lake, Mille Lacs, Red Lake, and White Earth Reservations, and Morton
Nebraska - Santee
New York State
North Dakota - Belcourt
South Dakota - Flandrau and Sisseton
Wisconsin - Bad River and Lac Courte Oreilles Reservations

Figure 8 Members of the Ojibway-Dakota Research Society of Minnesota. From "Ojibway and Dakota Place Names in Minnesota" (1963).[157]

Mary provided an overview of the committee that made decisions about which names would be included on the signs and how they would be spelled:

> We had created – it had been around in the past, but then we kind of revitalized or revived it – a bit of a cultural committee . . . Mike Swan was on that, and he used to be the Director of Natural Resources for many, many years. And then it was Larry Olson. Merlin. I think I got added on there because we were like, "We need to have a body to have some advisory on some of this stuff."[158]

During a summer 2021 interview, Mary Otto generously took the time to tell the story of how these signs emerged through the collaborative efforts of herself, White Earth Elders, knowledge-sharers, and an Ojibwe language speaker

157 Ojibway-Dakota Research Society of Minnesota (1963, p. 9). Image reproduced with permission of *The Minnesota Archaeologist* and the Minnesota Archaeological Society.

158 "Interview with Mary Otto," interview virtually conducted by Elan Pochedley, July 22, 2021.

critical to the project's development, Leonard "Sonny" McDougall. When I asked Mary about why the signs all focus on the names of different bodies of water at Gaa-waabaabiganikaag, she shared:

> At the time, there was – and still is – on the [Minnesota] Department of Transportation's website, guidance for signage, and it's for geographic locations. So I was like, "Oh, well I wanted to do geographic locations from the beginning, because, to me, we're about, as Anishinaabe, the connection of place, and the importance of water, and what you said are nonhuman relatives: those connections for our families and our students." So one, I guess, was it was easier from the state's perspective, or for legalities, or . . . state guidance.[159]

Under the Minnesota Department of Transportation's [MnDOT] Dakota and Ojibwe Language Signing Program, state regulations for road signs permitted Anishinaabemowin geographic markers for "lakes, rivers, streams, or creeks when that body of water is crossed by the trunk highway[,] by the use of a bridge [,] or the body of water is visible to the motorist."[160]

MnDOT allowing the installation of Anishinaabemowin signs would only be the first part in a complex process for selecting which names and waters received markers. Merlin conveyed to me that these signs were not cheap: "They're pretty expensive, 'cause you have to meet Roads, MnDOT, and federal specs. There's dimensions, the words, the lettering, it has to be in a certain font, and so forth. There's so many specifications that the engineers have to adhere to for the signage. So each sign probably costs right around $1,000 to get 'em up."[161] Due to these costs and the Minnesota Indian Affairs Council grant being for $12,000, where to place the signs would be thoughtfully addressed by the WEN cultural committee.[162]

Sonny McDougall remembered seeing a list of Anishinaabe place names for waters while in the Twin Cities, which set the committee on the path to locate the work of the Ojibway-Dakota Research Society. Recalling the progression of events, Mary shared: "[Sonny] said, 'You know, I think that we should start with the lakes. I remember seeing this book somewhere, long time ago.' He said, 'I feel like it came from the [Twin] Cities.' So I found the book, I found a reference, where he said it had the place names and the Ojibwe names for the water."[163] Sonny's interest reflected Anishinaabe people's attentiveness to

[159] "Interview with Mary Otto," interview virtually conducted by Elan Pochedley, July 22, 2021.
[160] MnDOT, "Dakota and Ojibwe Language Signing Program" (n.d., p. 2).
[161] "Interview with Merlin," interview conducted by Elan Pochedley, White Earth Reservation, August 2, 2017.
[162] *MnDOT Newsline* (2016).
[163] "Interview with Mary Otto," interview virtually conducted by Elan Pochedley, July 22, 2021.

and deeply meaningful relationships with bodies of water. On the significance of waters within and running through Gaa-waabaabiganikaag, Will Bement shared: "We use a lot of our waters for cultural resources, whether it be wild rice, netting, the fisheries, the leeching, even hunting for these things . . . "[164] Will, the WEN Fisheries Manager, also addressed the stakes and importance of protecting the waters of the reservation for future generations of White Earth Ojibwe, ensuring that they will have the option to exercise their treaty rights and participate in seasonal harvests:

> Well, for my job, you know just making sure that we have a sustainable resource out there. You know, what I don't want to see is people living in the now, where we might have really good fisheries today, but you never know in ten years, what it will be like for sustainability. That's what I'm looking out for. I want to make sure that my kids, when they make their choices, when they grow up, whether they're gonna exercise treaty rights or not, it'll be their choice. But I want to make sure that they have that option. I want to make sure they are able to net if they choose to do so. If they choose to rice, I want to make sure they have that chance to do it. I don't want our resources to get degraded so bad that they want to do it but they have no choice, they can't do it anymore because that resource is non-existent. So that's really, for my job, what I want to see or manage for. Just to make sure that my kids and their kids have a resource to be able to utilize.[165]

Anishinaabe members of the Ojibway-Dakota Research Society, such as Madison, traveled between the White Earth Reservation and the Twin Cities during their lifetimes, chronicling one place while living in the other. Similarly, Mary's tracking down of the collection of Ojibwe lake names remembered by Sonny demonstrates that these connections between Gaa-waabaabiganikaag and the Twin Cities continue into the present. Water was the medium and motivation which inspired the exchange of geographic knowledge and memory across generations of White Earth Ojibwe, both in the mid 1900s and in the twenty-first century.

Upon locating toponym lists created by the Ojibway-Dakota Research Society,[166] Mary constructed an approach for determining which place names to select for signs by asking cultural committee members to choose their top 20 locations. She communicated during our interview that committee members'

[164] "Interview with Will Bement," interview conducted by Elan Pochedley, White Earth Reservation, August 3, 2017.

[165] "Interview with Will Bement," interview conducted by Elan Pochedley, White Earth Reservation, August 3, 2017.

[166] Note: In an email communication on September 10, 2022, Mary Otto confirmed that the 1963 article published in *The Minnesota Archaeologist* that included place names recorded by the Ojibway-Dakota Research Society of Minnesota was the material she and Leonard "Sonny" McDougall used as the reference source for their Ojibwe language place name signage project.

Figure 9 Gaajikajiwe Gamaag sign. Photo by author.

criteria for choosing names concerned how frequently people passed respective waters, how old the recorded names were, and if lakes were used for seasonal activities such as the harvest of manoomin. Mary recalled the following responses she received when asking people, "Why did you pick that location?":

> "Well, I think this one's important because I drive by it every day." "Okay, that's a good reason." "There's a lot of traffic." "People go by there for work." "The bus goes by there." "It's one of the oldest names in the book that we found reference to." So there was all those conversations on choosing the names. "It's a lake people rice on." "It's a lake people harvest at a lot." "It's a lake that people . . . " We had the book and we just had all of our handwriting on it, just over and over [*Laughing*], on a map I wish I still had of White Earth.[167]

Ensuring that the signs would be seen by folks traveling across the reservation for school and work reflects Mary's original intention with the road markers, which was to create environmental print so that White Earth youth and people would witness how the Ojibwe language "is alive, it's still alive, and it's a living thing, and that it should be all around us – especially on our own lands."[168]

The scrutinizing and deconstructing of original Ojibwe place names and their meanings is a shared practice by both the White Earth Anishinaabeg involved with creating these modern-day signs and members of the Ojibway-Dakota

[167] "Interview with Mary Otto," interview virtually conducted by Elan Pochedley, July 22, 2021.
[168] "Interview with Mary Otto," interview virtually conducted by Elan Pochedley, July 22, 2021.

Research Society. The earlier Research Society based in Minneapolis claimed to "obtain and record such information as may be had, revealing the history and culture of the original people of the state"; this the collective achieved by focusing on the meanings of Ojibwe names and their accurate translations into English (see Figures 11–15).[169] Similarly, Mary discussed how the collaboration between Sonny McDougall, herself, and the other members of the cultural committee was a learning experience for gaining deeper understanding of Anishinaabemowin. Mary described how sharing space with Sonny gave her insights into geographic dimensions of the language:

> So I'm not proficient at all. I have things that just stick and I can read in Ojibwe, but just sitting with Sonny McDougall when he was still with us, I learned so much from him. Just like, having the *-ing* part of the word is location, and then having what you just described [about the meanings of waters' designations sometimes being distinct between Ojibwe and Euro-American names].[170]

Mary also shared how she saw these signs as educational tools, supporting those who know or are learning Anishinaabemowin, while also "help[ing] ask the question if they don't know language."[171]

When traversing the roads of Gaa-waabaabiganikaag, the signs mark the White Earth Reservation as an Ojibwe space (see Figure 9). As addressed in Section 4, Anishinaabemowin's presence via the signage – despite the lack of widespread knowledge of the language – has been interpreted as creating senses of belonging, of pride, of curiosity, and of personal disappointment for respective Anishinaabe interviewees. On the process of developing these markers, Mary recounted how the Ojibwe place names and meanings were delivered to the Minnesota Department of Transportation: "So I submitted that to them [MnDOT] from my conversations with Sonny and his translations and his meanings" (see Figure 10).[172] Rather than sending these Ojibwe toponyms and their English translations to the Minnesota Historical Society – as earlier chroniclers of Anishinaabemowin place names had done in the 1880s and 1940s[173] – creating visible, contemporary representations of these names at White Earth instead required submitting them to the state agency responsible for public roads, not public history.

[169] Madison (1957).
[170] "Interview with Mary Otto," interview virtually conducted by Elan Pochedley, July 22, 2021.
[171] "Interview with Mary Otto," interview virtually conducted by Elan Pochedley, July 22, 2021.
[172] "Interview with Mary Otto," interview virtually conducted by Elan Pochedley, July 22, 2021.
[173] Minnesota Historical Society (1944, p. 304); and, Minnesota Historical Society (1947, p. 374).

English	Ojibwe (phonetic)	Ojibwe (double vowel)	Meaning
Ice Cracking Lake	GahNahMahDwayQuaDing	Gaa-naamadwekwading	Traveling sound of cracking ice
Many Point Lake	GahMahMiNayMahNiWong	Gaa-maaminemaaniwang	Where there are many shore points
Strawberry Lake	GahoDahEneMeeKog	Gaa-ode'iminikaag	Where strawberries abound
Big Rat Lake	GahGeChiWahZhoshkoKog	Gaa-gichi-wazhaskokaag	Lake where muskrats are many
Juggler Lake	GeSahKonNing	Giisaakoning	Juggler of Medicine; his place of performance of medicine ceremony
Little Bemidji Lake	BayMeeGeGumMahSing	Bemijigamaasing	Small lake lying diagonally
White Earth Lake	GahWahBahBiGonEKagZahGahEGon	Gaawaabaabiganikaag zaaga'igan	Graying Clay Earth Lake
Pine Point	NayZhingWakOKong	Nezhingwaakokaang	Pines all over
Snider Lake	GeNeBayMeSounoceSeNon	Ginibemoozoonsinoon	Sleeping Little Moose
Island Lake	GahMinIsSeWong	Gaa-minisiwang	Lake of Islands
Green Water		Ozhaawashkobiig Zaaga'igan	
Buffalo River	MashKoDeBiShiKiZebe	Mashkode bizhiki ziibii	Bison/Buffalo stream/creek
Little Bass Lake	AhSheGonceSahGahEGun	Ashigaans Zaaga'igan	
Round Lake	GahWahWeYeaGumMog	Gaawaawiye Gamaag	Round body of water
Elbow Lake	GahoDosQuaNeeGumMog	Gaaodooskwaani Gamaag	Body of water shape of elbow
Elbow Lake Village		Gaaodooskwanni Gamaag Oodenawens	
Little Elbow Lake		Gaaodooskwanni Gamaagoonse	
Roy Lake	GahJahGeKugGeWayGomMog	Gaajikajiwe Gamaag	Lake enclosed by steep bluff banks
Perch Lake		Asaawe Zaaga'igan	
Tulaby Lake	OdeNeeBiSiKahNing	Odoonibii Zaaga'igan	Where tulabies abound
Rice Lake		Manoominakaazhiikaaning	
Net Lake		Asabikone Zaaga'igan	
Twin Lakes	GahNeeZhoGomMog	Gaaniizho Gamaag	Two lakes together

Figure 10 "Ojibwe Sign Translations."
List posted online by the Minnesota Department of Transportation.[174]

[174] MnDOT, "Ojibwe Sign Translations" (n.d.). Image reproduced with permission of White Earth Nation Research Review Board (WEN RRB).

BECKER COUNTY (cont.)

Tamarack Lake.
Ojibway - Gah-Mush-Ke-Qua-Tig-O-Kog.
Meaning - Tamarack forest.

Tulaby Lake.
Ojibway - O-De-Nee-Bi-Si-Kah-Ning.
Meaning - Where tulabies abound.

White Earth Lake.
Ojibway - Gah-Nah-Bah-Bi-Gon-E-Kag-Zah-Ga-E-Gon.
Meaning - Grayish clay earth lake.

Figure 11 Excerpt from *Report No. 1* by the Ojibway Research Society of Minnesota, April 1, 1944. Includes place names at Gaa-waabaabiganikaag. Image courtesy of the Minnesota Historical Society.[175]

MAHNOMEN COUNTY

Gull Lake.
Ojibway - Zah-Sha-Gein-Se-Kah-Ning.
Meaning - Where cranes are many.
(Named by Indians settled from the big Gull Lake.)

Island Lake.
Ojibway - Gah-Ne-Nes-Se-Wong.
Meaning - Lake of islands.

Roy Lake.
Ojibway - Gah-Jah-Ge-Kug-Ge-Way-Gom-Mog.
Meaning - Lake enclosed by steep bluff banks.

Snider Lake. (Previously known as Sucker Lake.)
Ojibway - Ge-Ne-Bah-Me-Sounce-Se-Non.
Meaning - Sleeping little moose. (Name given to Mrs. Snider
by Indians who lived at the lake.)

Figure 12 Excerpt from *Report No. 1* by the Ojibway Research Society of Minnesota, April 1, 1944. Includes place names at Gaa-waabaabiganikaag. Image courtesy of the Minnesota Historical Society.[176]

Figures 13 and 14 Views of the steep bluff banks from Gaajikajiwe Gamaag, Photos by author.

[175] Ojibway Research Society of Minnesota (1944, *Report No. 1*, p. 3).
[176] Ojibway Research Society of Minnesota (1944, *Report No. 1*, p. 5).

BECKER COUNTY (cont.)

Height Of Land Lake.
Ojibway - Ah-Sha-Way-Way-Se-Tah-Gen-Ning.
Meaning - Portage from body of water to another.

Ice Cracking Lake.
Ojibway- Gah-Nah-Mah-Dway-Qua-Ding.
Meaning - Traveling sound of cracking ice.

Island Lake.
Ojibway - Gah-Me-Nes-Se-Wong.
Meaning - Lake of islands.

Juggler Lake.
Ojibway - Ge-Sah-Kon-Ning.
Meaning - Juggler of Medicine. Medicine Man's place of performance of ceremony of medicine.

Little Bemidji Lake.
Ojibway - Bay-Mee-Ge-Gum-Mah-Sing.
Meaning - Small lake lying diagonally.

Little Flat Lake.
Ojibway- Nah-Dah-Gush-Kounce-Se-Kon-Ning.
Meaning - Flat rush lake.

Many Point Lake.
Ojibway - Gah-Mah-Mi-Nay-Mah-Ni-Wong.
Meaning - Where there are many shore points.

Round Lake.
Ojibway - Gah-Wah-We-Yea-Gum-Mog.
Meaning - Round body of water.

Shell Lake.
Ojibway - Gah-Ween-Bah-Ge-Way-Gom-Mog.
Meaning - Lake deep among hills.

Strawberry Lake.
Ojibway - Gah-O-Dah-E-Ne-Nee-Kog.
Meaning * Where strawberries abound.

Figure 15 Excerpt from *Report No. 1* by the Ojibway Research Society of Minnesota, April 1, 1944. Includes place names at Gaa-waabaabiganikaag. Image courtesy of the Minnesota Historical Society.[177]

[177] Ojibway Research Society of Minnesota (1944, *Report No. 1*, p. 2).

4 "We Want the Ojibwe on the Top. We're Not Renaming Something": The Politics of Names, Claims, and Returns

In this section, I address how the signs featuring Ojibwe toponyms for bodies of water have been interpreted by members of the WEN cultural committee, by White Earth Ojibwe people, and by select county commissioners. While two counties with overlapping jurisdictional claims with the White Earth Nation supported the installation of bilingual signs with Ojibwe place names appearing on top, two county commissioners of Becker County opposed the signs and this placement of the Anishinaabemowin toponyms. With these markers emerging out of the collaboration between the White Earth Nation and the Minnesota Department of Transportation, these signs present an example of a tangible way in which Indigenous knowledge, presence, and place names can be publicly respected and shared. In examining ethnographic interviews with White Earth personnel and citizens, I address Anishinaabe people's complex and diverse responses to the signs' creation and presence at Gaa-waabaabiganikaag. My analysis of their responses identifies the multiple associations these signs signify to community members who regularly pass them on reservation roads. Through these interviews, the comprehensibility of the Ojibwe language inscribed on these signs is addressed, both in the present and as positively envisioned in the future. I conclude with a brief discussion of how these Anishinaabemowin signs encourage viewers to engage with Ojibwe toponyms, investigate and understand their meanings, and hold relationships with the places they describe.

Navigating State Regulations and County Contestations

Road sign regulations by the Minnesota Department of Transportation (MnDOT), as well as resistance to the Anishinaabemowin signage by a couple of Becker County commissioners, initially posed obstacles to the installation of bilingual signs featuring Ojibwe place names at White Earth. Merlin recalled how this project required him and Mary to engage with various counties within the White Earth Reservation, as well as the state of Minnesota: "... White Earth is comprised of Becker, Mahnomen, and Clearwater counties. They wanted to hit the roads [for the signage project], so you have to go to each commission or roads department. And so when you do these things, you have to deal with the state, county, and federal government ..."[178] By navigating these requirements and working to develop positive relationships with the state agency responsible for regulating activities impacting public roads, White

178 "Interview with Merlin," interview conducted by Elan Pochedley, White Earth Reservation, August 2, 2017.

Earth personnel involved in this project were ultimately successful in getting these signs installed, with the Ojibwe place names on top.

During interviews with Merlin and Mary, they both stressed how they were committed to having the Ojibwe language designations above the English toponyms on the road signs. While he noted that the governments of "Clearwater and Mahnomen [counties] were no problem" in respect to installing the signs, Merlin described conflict with certain Becker County commissioners who were intent on placing the Ojibwe names below the English toponyms:

> One of the main things was [a couple of Becker County commissioners] didn't want Anishinaabemowin on top. They wanted English on top and they wanted the language on the bottom, but I argued with them . . . I said, "I want the Anishinaabe language on first and the English translation underneath." There was two board members in Becker County here that were really opposed to it . . .[179]

Here we see a couple commissioners of a county government – whose claimed jurisdictional boundaries are partially within the White Earth Reservation – attempting to exert their authority over signs constructed by an Ojibwe nation who originally secured the space of the reservation under an 1867 treaty with the US federal government. This story illuminates tensions between an Indigenous nation and a county government rooted in competing claims over the regulation of space and signage. A 2016 *Star Tribune* article included Becker County Commissioner Ben Grimsley's response to the markers: "A native person on reservation property has different hunting and fishing rights than they do on non-native property . . . So, if it all gets signed with Ojibwe, it would probably appear to be on the reservation."[180] He is also referenced in a 2016 *Detroit Lakes Tribune* article, with the author stating, "Becker County Commissioner Ben Grimsley expressed . . . that people might mistakenly think the land is tribal land. He said the Ojibwe-signed land may confuse some people and would be a problem especially when it comes to hunting on the land and such. He said he would rather see the English translation on top as well."[181] For Commissioner Grimsley, the installation of the Anishinaabemowin signs throughout the White Earth Reservation was associated with a fear that the markers would create an "appearance" that one is within the territory of Ojibwe people. In his statement, this Becker County official failed to acknowledge enduring Ojibwe on- and off-reservation rights to hunt, fish, and gather.

179 "Interview with Merlin," interview conducted by Elan Pochedley, White Earth Reservation, August 2, 2017.

180 Ross (2016). 181 Mayfield (2016).

In summer 2021, Mary described how, by refusing to change her stance on the position of the Ojibwe names, she successfully effected the signs we see today with the Anishinaabemowin situated above the English. She shared with me:

> We had the argument about the Ojibwe being on the top or bottom. We wanted it on the top. They wanted it smaller. They wanted it below. They didn't want to confuse people. I'm like, "Well let's do some historical markers. Let's put it on digital maps, that if you see the sign, you click on this icon and it'll tell you exactly . . . " "I don't think that people are gonna be confused that it's a lake. I don't think people are gonna be confused that . . . " So we went round and round. You saw what we ended up with. It wasn't [finished] on time, but it was well worth the push and holding on tight.[182]

Why face all this adversity to have the Ojibwe on the top instead of the bottom? What does the presence of one above the other signify for those behind the project? Mary addressed these questions in a 2016 *Star Tribune* interview, wherein she said, "We want the Ojibwe on the top. We're not renaming something. That's what it was originally called on our land by the people who lived here."[183] Although these personnel of White Earth were "not renaming something," they certainly were making visible, through intentional decisions and spatial commitments, environmental print throughout the reservation that centered the language and geographic knowledge of their Anishinaabe ancestors, and, increasingly in recent years, their youth (see Figure 16).

According to Merlin, the first attempt to place the road signs in the soils of Gaa-waabaabiganikaag was met with resistance by Becker County officials: "So Becker County sent the letter addressed to, I guess addressed to me. It came to me, but it came to the Legal Department and the Executive Director, and they said that they were gonna tear [down] the signs, take 'em down. It was just a big mess. I had to meet with . . . our Environment and Roads Department and our lawyer and so forth."[184] One of the initially installed signs was taken down by a county transportation office, but not for reasons aligned with certain Becker County commissioners' fight against the Ojibwe names appearing on top. Rather, the support structures weren't in compliance with MnDOT requirements (see Figure 17). Following is a full retelling by Mary of the events that led to the removal of an Ojibwe language sign:

> We didn't run into issues with our Tribal Council; it was with the county transportation offices. So I just looked for a sign company. I was like, "Hey, I have these signs I want to do and they're gonna be really big because they're in

[182] "Interview with Mary Otto," interview virtually conducted by Elan Pochedley, July 22, 2021.

[183] Ross (2016).

[184] "Interview with Merlin," interview conducted by Elan Pochedley, White Earth Reservation, August 2, 2017.

Figure 16 Odoonibii Zaaga'igan sign. Photo by author.

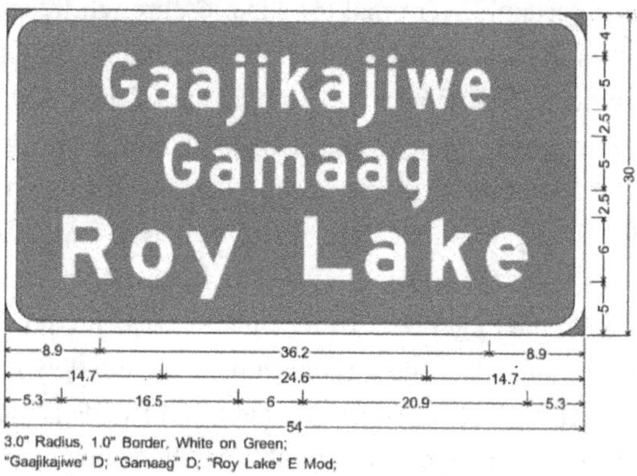

Figure 17 Sign design example for Minnesota Department of Transportation's "Dakota and Ojibwe Language Signing Program."[185]

Ojibwe and our words are long because they're descriptive." And they're like, "Sure. We've done different road signs for people." So I looked up all these things . . . Oh, it has to be made standard. It has to be a certain amount reflective or something. You know, I'm an educator, so I'm not [familiar with the regulations for roads signs]. So I remember going to work and getting a call, "Mary, someone took one of your signs down." Like, "Excuse me?!" [*Laughing*] Like, "What do you mean?" "First of all, they're not *my* signs. What do you mean?"

[185] MnDOT, "Dakota and Ojibwe Language Signing Program" (n.d., p. 4). Image reproduced with permission of White Earth Nation RRB.

> "Someone from the county took one of our signs down." How can the county come on our reservation, on our reservation roads, and take a sign down? Well it turns out that Minnesota Department of Transportation had some regulations around signs that I was not aware of. I didn't go on their website or think I should talk to those people, because it was within the confines of the reservation. So at least one part of the answer to your question is: At the time, there was – and still is – on the [Minnesota] Department of Transportation's website, guidance for signage, and it's for geographic locations.[186]

Mary described how the state's concerns were based on regulations and the safety of those traveling on the roadways, as well as how this episode ultimately culminated in a partnership between herself and MnDOT officials:

> So when I found out that they took the sign down and I called and was told, "It's way too big." "The legs holding the sign are not up to standard of . . . " "We have this much distance from the road." "Our Tribal Roads Department put the signs up." "Well, because it's this type of road and this much traffic on it, it needs to be this kind where if a car hits it, it breaks at a certain point." I was like, "Oh, of course. I should've known that." [*Laughing*] But after learning more about the process on that from the DOT [MnDOT] . . . They were terrific! So they came. They were like, "Hey Mary, we heard you have a problem!" [*Laughing*] And so, we worked through it with their support from their Tribal staff at DOT. And then I started traveling, doing a little bit of language work and sign work with Department of Transportation at conferences, talking about the sign project, along with Jason Hollinday from Fond du Lac.[187]

This unanticipated interruption to the project illustrates how this rejection of an Ojibwe place name marker was not based in efforts to suppress Native knowledges and spatial representation. Instead, this specific situation reveals that when you're putting signs on roads, you must be attentive to safety regulations.

The advocacy work of Mary and Merlin translated into the Minnesota Department of Transportation assisting the White Earth Band of Ojibwe with installing environmental print for the benefit of Anishinaabe youth and community members (see Figure 18).[188] Merlin shared his primary motivation for being involved with the signage project:

> It took probably nine months, and . . . there was articles in the paper and so forth. I got a lot of calls, people wanting to do interviews, but I didn't really want to do interviews because that's not the intent. My intent is to preserve our language for our young kids and our youth to be proud of who they are and to see the language day-to-day, 'cause they have to see the language.[189]

186 "Interview with Mary Otto," interview virtually conducted by Elan Pochedley, July 22, 2021.
187 "Interview with Mary Otto," interview virtually conducted by Elan Pochedley, July 22, 2021.
188 *Anishinaabeg Today* (2016, p. 1); and, *MnDOT Newsline* (2016).
189 "Interview with Merlin," interview conducted by Elan Pochedley, White Earth Reservation, August 2, 2017.

ANISHINAABEG TODAY

A Monthly Chronicle of the White Earth Nation

Vol. 21 No. 12 White Earth, Minn. today@whiteearth-nsn.gov Wednesday, November 2, 2016

A new 'Sign' of the times...

Photo by Jerimiah Moerke

White Earth Reservation and the Minnesota Department of Transportation (MnDOT) recently worked together to place Ojibwe/English language signs in several locations in Becker and Mahnomen Counties, including along Highway 59 north of Callaway. The new signs were provided by White Earth, and the Minnesota Department of Transportation provided the posts and installed them. This was made possible through a grant from the Minnesota Indian Affairs Council, thanks to a legislative appropriation to preserve the arts and cultural heritage of Minnesota. Appropriated grant money is "to preserve Dakota and Ojibwe Indian languages and to foster educational programs in Dakota and Ojibwe languages." From left are Dean Kroulik - MnDOT District 4 signs, Doug Bergquist - MnDOT District 4 signs, Jeff DeHaan - MnDOT District 4 sign supervisor, and Jeff Vivier - White Earth Reservation Public Works director.

Stocking sturgeon

White Earth officials following 20-year plan

White Earth Reservation recently released 3,000 seven to eight inch sturgeon in White Earth Lake, and 1,900 seven to eight inch sturgeon in Round Lake. Around 10,800 seven to eight inch sturgeon were released along sections of the Wild Rice River.

White Earth has a 20-year management strategy in coordination with the United States Fish and Wildlife Service (USFWS) and Rainy River First Nations (Canada). White Earth is currently in the 17th year.

Over the years, stocking numbers have been adjusted to accommodate for success rates of the sturgeon. The staff just recently completed a sturgeon survey on White Earth and Round Lake with assistance from the USFWS.

Top left: COLA 5th graders Brooke Barrett, left, and Anjel Fineday help release sturgeon. **Top right:** WE Natural Resources staff member Tim Lafriniere holding a sturgeon on Round Lake. **Left:** WE Fisheries staff members Gerald Roberts, left, and Cliff Crowell collecting sturgeon data.

Submitted photos

Figure 18 "A New 'Sign' of the Times," article in *Anishinaabeg Today*, November 2, 2016.[190]

With these signs present, visible, and installed with the support of MnDOT, White Earth youth have been seeing these place names for nearly a decade now, as they travel throughout Gaa-waabaabiganikaag (see Figure 19).

White Earth Community Responses

The following ethnographic interview excerpts demonstrate how these signs have been interpreted by White Earth Nation citizens, descendants, and personnel as emanating an affective sense of home, restoring connections to the language that contest narratives of *complete loss* (referencing Mishuana Goeman's writing),[191] supporting the building of an environment where the language is increasingly observed, and helping the Ojibwe of White Earth envision and realize a future where their children will fluently speak Anishinaabemowin, preserving it through active engagement. In this section,

[190] *Anishinaabeg Today* (2016, p. 1). Image reproduced with permission of White Earth Nation RRB.

[191] Goeman (2013, p. 180).

Figure 19 Gaa-maaminemaaniwang sign. Photo by author.

I focus on how White Earth citizens and descendants who live on or visit the reservation have interpreted the meaning of the Ojibwe signage.

Drawing on ethnographic evidence, I argue that the *presences* of the Ojibwe place names represented on the signs play a significant role in gradually resurrecting a shared linguistic environment rooted in relationships with waters for the White Earth Ojibwe. The collective memory of the language displayed upon the place name signs constructs a temporal linkage between the past, present, and future. The contemporary inheritance of these names was made possible through their preservation by an earlier generation of Ojibwe people, many from White Earth, who gathered in Minneapolis throughout the 1940s and 1950s. By preserving geographic knowledge, names, and meanings, members of the Ojibway-Dakota Research Society ensured they *could* be remembered, even if society members were not aware of *how* that knowledge would later be utilized.

Merlin discussed how these signs restore the original place names for respective waters. On the authenticity of these names, he elaborated: "So the names are original. A lot of the names, like on 59 here, the Buffalo River [is] 'Mashkode bizhiki'. Round Lake, East Lake, Roy Lake, Net Lake, White Earth . . . Them are the original names of the lakes here that the Tribe has always had. We just got the signs for that and put 'em up."[192] The recent visual

[192] "Interview with Merlin," interview conducted by Elan Pochedley, White Earth Reservation, August 2, 2017.

emergence of names previously widely known and spoken by past generations of Ojibwe, in a certain sense, returns the meanings of bodies of water that Anishinaabe people had historically observed and/or attributed to these places. These "meanings" are not reducible to observers recognizing or comprehending the designations in Anishinaabemowin; rather, they are also deeply rooted in the restoration of ancestral relationships between the names, the waters, and the Ojibwe. I argue that these signs restore Ojibwe people's linguistic, spatial, and environmental relationships that were previously interrupted by Indian boarding, mission, and day schools, as well as the large-scale territorial dispossession of the Anishinaabeg of White Earth.

The literal meanings of many of these waters' names are also returned through the presence of the signs. The re-emergence of these place names that preceded Euro-American settlement of this region also corrects identities of places that have lost dimensions of their meaning due to anglicization or outright replacement. Perhaps the clearest example from those bodies of water selected for the signage project, Roy Lake's original name is Gaajikajiwe Gamaag which means "Lake enclosed by steep bluff banks." Other names have more nuanced distinctions with Ice Cracking Lake's original Ojibwe name being Gaa-naamadwekwading, meaning, "Travelling sound of cracking ice," and Big Rat Lake's original name, Gaa-gichi-wazhaskokaag, meaning "Lake where muskrats are many."[193]

While some names share similar meanings between Ojibwe and English designations, the Anishinaabemowin name for Snider Lake, Ginibemoozoonsinoon, translates to "Sleeping little moose."[194] One might initially interpret this as an English toponym displacing an Indigenous place name derived from observational knowledge. However, investigation into this specific lake and its toponymic history tells a different story. According to Ed Crane's 1947 article about the Ojibway-Dakota Research Society, "They discovered that Mrs. Snider, wife of an early pioneer, was well and affectionately known by the Indians. That, in fact, she had been dubbed by them 'Little Sleeping Moose.' What's more, they discovered why she'd been given this nickname. It seems that Mrs. Snider snored at night."[195] While the origins of Ginibemoozoonsinoon are likely humorous and aren't attributable – as far as we can tell – to the presence or the story of a young moose at the lake, we can deduce that there was a possibility that the Ojibwe of White Earth were aware that moose do, in fact, snore! Further, the initial 1944 report of the Ojibway-Dakota Research Society (then known as the Ojibway Research Society of Minnesota) asserts that the previous name for Ginibemoozoonsinoon was

[193] MnDOT, "Ojibwe Sign Translations" (n.d.).
[194] MnDOT, "Ojibwe Sign Translations" (n.d.). [195] Crane (1947).

"Nah-May-Be-Ne-Kah-Wing" which translates to "Lake of many suckers."[196] This demonstrates that lakes could have more than one name, speaking to different features and/or narratives of place and that the earlier designation for this lake was connected to the presence of, a story concerning, and/or an event relating to other-than-humans, being sucker fish.

Contemporarily, the signs have returned the meanings of these places in an unconventional sense. To observe the meanings articulated within the names on the markers, one would need to be able to read and understand the Ojibwe words depicted. With the White Earth Nation's current fluency rate being below 1 percent – according to Chairman Fairbanks –, the linguistic meanings of these toponyms are likely to be missed by the majority of those passing the geographic markers.[197] In a July 2017 interview, Jill Doerfler (White Earth Anishinaabe), who grew up in Mahnomen and is not fluent in the language, stressed the signs' striking presence on the reservation: "So yeah, I like seeing the signs when I go home now. And they're large, because the Ojibwe words are long. So you can't miss it, which is good. It is an intimidating language."[198] Jill told me how she sees the signs as a reminder of the White Earth Nation's jurisdiction on reservation land, while also being a potential source of insecurity for those Anishinaabeg who do not understand the language. On how she personally perceives the relationship between the signs, history of language loss, and exposure to Anishinaabemowin for all people living or traveling within the boundaries of the reservation, Jill shared:

> So I think, in a way, it's awesome because it highlights White Earth immediately; a kind of identifier that you're on Native land. But because Anishinaabe language fluency is low, I also have to wonder if other people don't also feel sort of like, "Well, how many White Earth people can pronounce those words?" Hopefully more as generations go on, but I think it could bring up that kind of like disappointment or feeling of inadequacy in some ways.[199]

With the Ojibwe language being targeted and suppressed within Indian boarding, mission, and day schools, it is not hard to imagine how a "feeling of inadequacy" could overcome a viewer passing the visual articulation of a language and a name they would have plausibly understood without these institutions' concerted efforts to eliminate Anishinaabemowin.

[196] Ojibway Research Society of Minnesota (1944, *Report No. 1*, pp. 10–11).

[197] *Anishinaabeg Today* (2022, p. 9).

[198] "Interview with Jill Doerfler," interview conducted by Elan Pochedley, Duluth, Minnesota, July 25, 2017.

[199] "Interview with Jill Doerfler," interview conducted by Elan Pochedley, Duluth, Minnesota, July 25, 2017. Includes additions submitted on February 6, 2025.

Will Bement similarly asserted that the signage makes it clear that you are driving through Ojibwe territory. He told me: "It's nice to see that, just to know that you *are* on Anishinaabe land. It's just nice to see that kind of thing. It just gives people a reminder, you know: this is where we're at, this is where we come from, and this is our culture. And it's nice to see those things. You know?"[200] Jill concurred with Will, asserting that these Anishinaabemowin signs portray historic Ojibwe connections to Gaa-waabaabiganikaag, while also demonstrating the contemporary presences of the Indigenous people of White Earth on their own reservation. She said, "I think that's a nice marker that our ancestors, Native people, had names for these places! These places weren't just named and discovered when non-Native settlers came into the area . . . I would hope it creates an awareness for non-Natives, because there is so much erasure at White Earth of the [Ojibwe] Nation."[201]

Will conveyed that he views the signs as a source of pride in communicating Ojibwe identity and Anishinaabe geographic belonging. Like Jill's sentiments, he noted how the low fluency rate may shape experiences with the signs:

> . . . if you see those things it might trigger someone to ask a question to their grandparents, "What does that mean?" You know, "I've seen this lake was called this, what does that mean?" Or "What's the significance of it?" "Why do they call it that, is there a reason?" Or "Was that a family name?" You know, it triggers questions for people to ask, which is a good thing.[202]

Both Jill and Will noted how the signs distinguish this space as Ojibwe territory, while also observing how widespread knowledge of Anishinaabemowin is largely not present within the White Earth Reservation. However, these two interviewees differed in how they envision the consequences of these markers for those citizens and descendants of White Earth who do not currently speak the language.

Jacob Syverson, White Earth's Land Analyst, discussed how he sees the combination of low Ojibwe language fluency and the presence of the place name signs as creating desires to investigate the meanings surrounding respective designations:

> I think that's fantastic. I think they should have more of that. Just because there's so many White Earth members that I know – no one knows any Ojibwe words or what [places are] called. I think it's cool because it gets

[200] "Interview with Will Bement," interview conducted by Elan Pochedley, White Earth Reservation, August 3, 2017.

[201] "Interview with Jill Doerfler," interview conducted by Elan Pochedley, Duluth, Minnesota, July 25, 2017.

[202] "Interview with Will Bement," interview conducted by Elan Pochedley, White Earth Reservation, August 3, 2017.

> people asking questions. You know, like "Hey, what does that say?" "I don't know!" "We'll have to look it up!"[203]

Jill shared related thoughts when she discussed the significance of the names beyond their symbolic value as representations of the Ojibwe language throughout the reservation. Jill articulated the role she hopes these signs will have in the future: "And so I hope that's what they think of; not only that those places had names, but that maybe as language revitalization comes through, we can start using those names, those Anishinaabe names again in the future."[204] As each of these interlocutors conveyed, the signs are not only valuable in marking the reservation as Ojibwe space; they also hold meanings waiting to be understood – by future generations of fluent speakers or by those who grow curious to investigate the Ojibwe place names printed on sheet aluminum that they pass every day on their way to school/work, and on their way home.

After seeing these signs, I was disappointed by the lack of information about the Ojibwe place names or their meanings posted online. It took me years to eventually track down an Excel sheet of names and translations posted by the Minnesota Department of Transportation.[205] Despite being Potawatomi/ Neshnabé and from a different Fire of the Council of Three Fires, I personally desired to learn more about the signs and Anishinaabemowin toponyms after having passed them on the roads of White Earth, as evidenced in the interview footage and archival research featured throughout this Element.

How did Mary imagine these signs' future significance for White Earth youth and community members when their meanings were hidden despite being in plain sight? She articulated that the markers may serve as a platform for future instruction, not just for the White Earth youth learning the Ojibwe language in their classrooms. Mary described how she would like to see the knowledge surrounding and contained within these names further presented to all those traveling throughout the reservation and witnessing these postings. She expressed hope that future programming would address "What the name means, why it was named that, what happened at those sites, why it's important, and some history on it for our own people and for all people in Minnesota or people who drive through our territories."[206] Here, Mary articulates a vision for educating Ojibwe people and the wider public on the source of these names,

203 "Interview with Jacob Syverson," interview virtually conducted by Elan Pochedley, July 12, 2021.

204 "Interview with Jill Doerfler," interview conducted by Elan Pochedley, Duluth, Minnesota, July 25, 2017.

205 MnDOT, "Ojibwe Sign Translations" (n.d.).

206 "Interview with Mary Otto," interview virtually conducted by Elan Pochedley, July 22, 2021.

what occurred at these sites, and why they are or were significant to the White Earth Anishinaabeg.

Reflecting Mary's guiding purpose for installing the signs – to create environmental print in the Ojibwe language for Tribal youth learning Anishinaabemowin and for other White Earth people –, Megan Bakken spoke of their role in the linguistic development of her children. In having kids who have gone through the Ojibwe language program at the local Head Start, she noted the importance of the signage for learning and comprehending Anishinaabemowin: "But with them learning it too, it should help preserve it. *And then over time, some of them can even start reading some of the signs*, so that's kind of cool ... It's kind of a reminder, I guess, on preserving the language."[207] The language choice of "preservation" is significant, because, at first glance, it appears to solely reflect that Anishinaabemowin is threatened by low fluency rates; however, in addition to this meaning, preservation of the language is a long-standing practice of the White Earth Ojibwe, with historic efforts to document Anishinaabemowin place names enabling their recent revival throughout Gaa-waabaabiganikaag. Further, with Megan not having access to Anishinaabemowin lessons in public school when growing up, her current education in the Anishinaabe language is made possible through public road signs and her own children. On the latter, she pointed out: "But now the kids have the option of learning Ojibwe. And they learn it from Head Start, so [with] all my little kids, I'm actually learning little bits."[208]

Conclusion

These road signs depict Ojibwe presence in greater detail and depth than merely the representational importance of Anishinaabemowin signs being visible on the reservation, although there is significance in this as well. Whether the meanings of the names on these signs are comprehended or not, their visual presentation creates "environmental print" that depicts Ojibwe environmental knowledge through the meanings of the names themselves. Ojibwe environmental knowledge and Anishinaabemowin are directly related through place-based names and relationships spanning Gaa-waabaabiganikaag. The visual appearance of these Ojibwe toponyms via signage demonstrates the survivance and endurance of Ojibwe people, their language, their memory of place, and their worldviews rooted in natural reason (to reference Vizenor).[209] With these

[207] "Interview with Megan Bakken," interview conducted by Elan Pochedley, White Earth Reservation, July 20, 2017.

[208] "Interview with Megan Bakken," interview conducted by Elan Pochedley, White Earth Reservation, July 20, 2017.

[209] Vizenor (2009, p. 88).

names becoming increasingly legible for more and more Ojibwe people as White Earth youth continue their education in Anishinaabemowin, I speculate that meaningful associations with these place names and the bodies of water they describe will continue to grow. In February 2025, Megan shared that her children are learning the Ojibwe language at an on-reservation public school that she herself attended prior to Anishinaabemowin being offered. Megan informed me that Ojibwe language lessons and classes are also currently taught through multiple White Earth Head Start programs and Boys & Girls Clubs across Gaa-waabaabiganikaag. As a result of these efforts, I anticipate that the meanings of these names will become comprehensible for a growing number of White Earth Anishinaabe people, being understood through Anishinaabe worldviews communicated through the Ojibwe language and through ongoing connections to these waters of significance.

As discussed in Section 3, the White Earth cultural committee placed the signs along roads where people frequently traveled, for places of collective significance, and for waters with the oldest Ojibwe toponyms. I suggest that the creation and observation of these road signs draws on – perhaps inadvertently, perhaps not – two central elements of the Ojibwe seasonal round: (1) migration/mobility; and, (2) place-based observation and knowledge. Ojibwe people's common routes along roads and highways across the reservation – in traveling to school, to work, and so on – created a formula for the White Earth cultural committee to determine which sites would have their names represented on signs. As previously addressed, Anishinaabe aki– Anishinaabe territory – has been constituted by seasonal returns/departures, environmental knowledges, place-based relationships, and governing protocols of Ojibwe people across generations. These signs provide a unique map of Gaa-waabaabiganikaag as Ojibwe space, with the visual names in the language tying the water- and land-scapes of White Earth together. Interestingly, one needs to be present near the waters in order to observe their respective names. This dual observation – of Ojibwe toponyms communicating environmental features and of the bodies of water themselves – embeds Anishinaabemowin within the visual plane of the reservation, while also ensuring that these place names are learned in geographic contexts in which they hold value: in the presence of the bodies they describe. These signs were created by the White Earth cultural committee to instill pride in Ojibwe youth and to ensure their language is recognized as being alive. I posit that these toponyms and their presentation on the signs also articulate an endurance of Ojibwe territoriality in the continuing transmission of intergenerational geographic knowledge through the ongoing movements and environmental observations of Anishinaabe people.

5 Roots in White Clay: A Pre-Reservation History of Gaa-waabaabiganikaag

Responses to the road signs addressed in Section 4 allow us to identify a tension concerning *whose* space was interpreted as being marked by the bilingual signs throughout Gaa-waabaabiganikaag. The varying responses the signs elicited demonstrate that differing constructions and perceptions of space can publicly collide when linguistic landscapes are transformed in visual, textual, and tangible ways. With criticisms of the recently installed Anishinaabemowin signs revolving around claims that reservation lands and waters are not places of Ojibwe rights, authority, or governance, this section offers an intervention rooted in historic harvests, encounters, migrations, navigations, and memories. I illustrate long-standing Anishinaabe presences at Gaa-waabaabiganikaag and neighboring areas by following archival traces of Ojibwe geographic knowledge, navigational prowess, seasonal returns and harvests, expressions of hospitality, assertions of governing authority, and toponyms recorded in early nineteenth-century maps. In doing so, I present what Madeline Whetung refers to as the "deep geographies" of the area surrounding and encapsulating Gaa-waabaabiganikaag prior to the reservation's creation.[210]

Historic Cartographic Representations and Ojibwe Toponyms

Maps featuring Ojibwe place names and borders present an avenue for tracing Anishinaabe people's spatial relationships and geographic knowledge before the creation of the White Earth Reservation in 1867. According to Melissa Meyer, the 1,296 square miles[211] that became the White Earth Reservation was a "previously uninhabited buffer zone over which Dakota and Anishinaabeg had competed for generations, creating a sort of game preserve."[212] In her otherwise meticulous history of the reservation's development, Meyer describes this area as "uninhabited" prior to 1867, largely ignoring the histories and names of the region presented shortly. *White Earth: A History* (1989) describes Dakota returns to this area of their historical and ancestral belonging. In this work, the White Earth Reservation Curriculum Committee describes the Mississippi Bands of Ojibwe's early migrations to Gaa-waabaabiganikaag being marked by the threat of Dakota returns: "Bands of hostile Dakota sometimes returned to north-central Minnesota."[213] In this section, I will remedy Meyer's characterization of this region as being previously uninhabited by chronicling Ojibwe presence, authority, hospitality, seasonal harvests, and geographic knowledge concerning

210 Whetung (2016, p. 110). 211 White Earth Nation, "Natural Resources" (n.d.).
212 Meyer (1999, p. 226).
213 White Earth Reservation Curriculum Committee et al. (1989, p. 28).

Gaa-waabaabiganikaag and nearby regions in the decades preceding the reservation's creation.

Early to mid nineteenth-century maps depict geographic knowledge of Ojibwe and Dakota peoples and nations, refuting Meyer's language of the land base of the White Earth Reservation being a "previously uninhabited buffer zone" prior to 1867. In making the following observations, I am *not* presenting any claims concerning the borders between Ojibwe and Dakota territories, *nor* am I suggesting that we should uncritically accept the following cartographic representations of place names by Beltrami, Allen, and Nicollet as offering objective truth(s); the situated knowledges, specific perspectives, worldviews, and potential biases of mapmakers and their informants should call claims of cartographic objectivity into doubt. However, these maps reveal inscribed presences of Ojibwe and Dakota people through the appearance of toponyms in their respective languages, as well as in the presentation of their English translations.

Giacomo Costantino Beltrami's 1827 map presents the region along the Red River of the North, considered part of the Otter Tail River within this map (see Figure 20). Beltrami collected cartographic data during his travels throughout

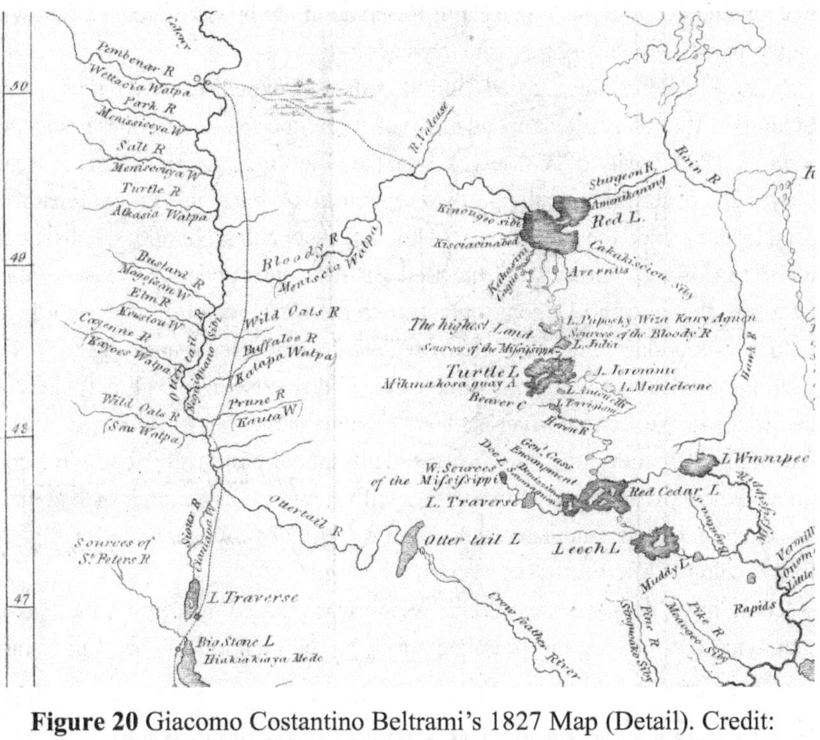

Figure 20 Giacomo Costantino Beltrami's 1827 Map (Detail). Credit: University of Minnesota, John R. Borchert Map Library.[214]

[214] Beltrami (1827, map).

Dakota and Ojibwe territories during the 1820s.[215] The Otter Tail River included in Beltrami's map was located west and south of the forthcoming White Earth Reservation. The area surrounding this river includes both Dakota and Ojibwe place names for bodies of water. Of note is the abundance of Dakota toponyms along the Otter Tail River, while the name of the river itself is presented in Ojibwe, being "Neguiquano Sibi." This same central body of water was later recorded in Gilfillan's 1885 collection of Ojibwe place names as "Nigigwanowe-zibi."[216] Beltrami describes different Ojibwe and Dakota names existing for this waterway:

> This then into which the Sioux river falls, is not the Red river, but the river *Neguiquanosibi*, as the Cypowais [Chippewas] call it, or the river of the Otter's-tail, from its having its source in the lake of that name. The Sioux [Dakota] know it under the name *Kakaweuapi-Watpà*, or the river of the Falls, from the number of them which occur on its issuing from the lake.[217]

Despite the Otter Tail River flowing largely outside of the forthcoming boundaries of the White Earth Reservation, the headwaters of Neguiquano Sibi's watershed were, and are, located at Gaa-waabaabiganikaag.[218] In Beltrami's cartographic record of this region published in 1827, additional lakes and rivers to the east of what would become the White Earth Reservation are primarily represented with names in the Ojibwe and English languages.

In James Allen's map created following an 1832 expedition with Henry Rowe Schoolcraft,[219] the lieutenant and mapmaker includes boundary lines associated with the 1825 Treaty of Prairie du Chien (see Figure 21). Article 5 of the treaty provided a description of the borders separating Ojibwe and Dakota territories established under the agreement.[220] In Joseph Nicolas Nicollet's subsequent map (1843), we can see how the Red River is surrounded by Ojibwe place names to the east and Dakota toponyms to the west, seemingly in accordance with the boundary lines depicted on Allen's map (see Figure 22). This is exemplified through a Dakota name for a wild rice river – "psihn" (psíŋ) – to the west of the central river and an Ojibwe name for a wild rice river – "manomin" (manoomin) – to the east. This spatial pattern for toponyms continues when we zoom out from that detail to cover a larger area of Nicollet's map, which includes names of lakes and rivers that would be found within the forthcoming White Earth Reservation (see Figure 23).

These maps demonstrate that this region was marked by Ojibwe and Dakota toponyms and geographic presences prior to the creation of the White Earth

[215] Beltrami (1828). [216] Gilfillan (1885, p. 463); and, Upham (1920, p. 390).
[217] Beltrami (1828, p. 335).
[218] Minnesota Pollution Control Agency, "Otter Tail River" (n.d.). [219] Mason (1993).
[220] "Treaty with the Sioux, etc., 1825" (1825).

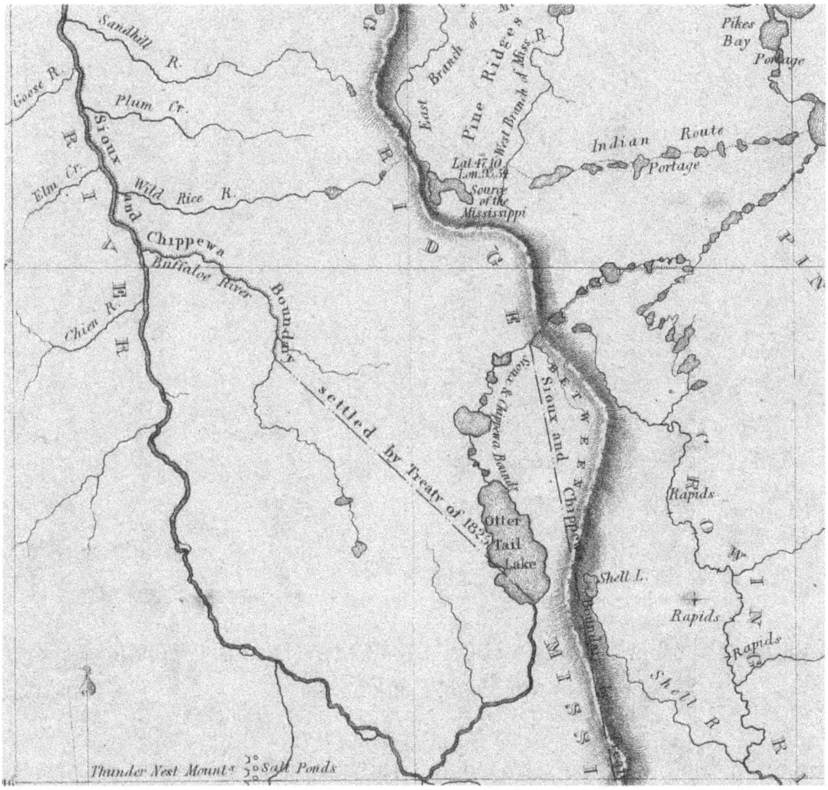

Figure 21 James Allen's 1832 Map (Detail). Credit: University of Minnesota, John R. Borchert Map Library.[221]

Reservation. From my limited investigations of related expedition notes, reports, and publications,[222] I could not identify how each of these cartographers and their teams made decisions about which/whose names to depict, which/whose language to use for specific toponyms, which informants' geographic knowledges to prioritize, and, generally speaking, who informants were.[223] An exception is found in Nicollet's journals from 1836 to 1837, wherein hints of potential informants are made, including guides Chagobay (Ojibwe), Kégouédgikâ/ Kegwedzissag (Ojibwe), and Brunia (Ojbwe/French).[224] In presenting these cartographic representations published between 1827 and 1843, I've challenged

[221] Allen (1832, map).

[222] Beltrami (1828); U.S. War Department et al. (1834); Mason (1993); Nicollet (1836/1970); and, Nicollet (1843, report).

[223] Cole and Hart (2021).

[224] Nicollet (1836/1970, pp. 34, 46, 85–86, 88, 90, 127); Nicollet (1843, p. 60); Northern Community Radio – KAXE & KBXE, "Our History: The Journey of Chagobay and Brunia – Ten-part series," Part 7 (2012); and, Northern Community Radio – KAXE & KBXE, "Our History: The Journey of Chagobay and Brunia – Ten-part series," Part 10 (2012).

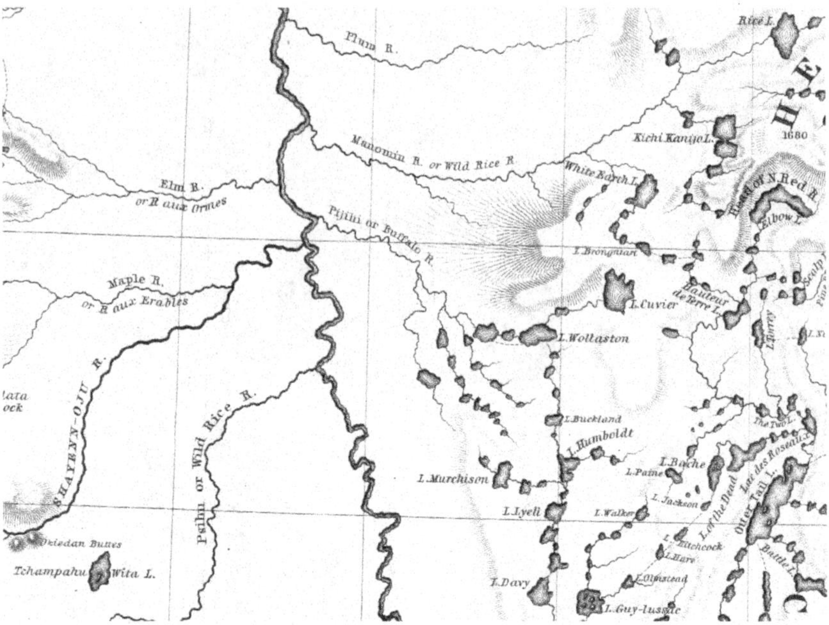

Figure 22 Joseph Nicolas Nicollet's 1843 Map (Detail). Credit: University of Michigan, Clark Library.[225]

the claim that the region surrounding Gaa-waabaabiganikaag was uninhabited and without territorial relationships prior to 1867.

Nicollet's 1843 map evidences Ojibwe environmental knowledge of the features of Gaa-waabaabiganikaag decades prior to the creation of the reservation. Names depicting Anishinaabe environmental observations and other-than-human presences include the Ojibwe name for the Wild Rice River (being "Manomin R."), "White Earth L.," and "Kitchi Kanijo L." We can deduce that the Anishinaabeg who shared these names with Nicollet in 1836 were aware that this was a place of white clay (in reference to "White Earth Lake") and that "Kitchi Kanijo L[ake]" (spelled on the 2016 road sign as "Gaaniizho Gamaag"[226] and recorded by the Ojibway Research Society in 1944 as "Gah-Nee-Zho-Gom-Mog")[227] was the place of "two lakes together." These appearances of Anishinaabemowin toponyms, as well as a reference to white clay, offer evidence of Ojibwe people's preexisting relationships with waterways of Gaa-waabaabiganikaag prior to the creation of the White Earth Reservation.

225 Nicollet et al. (1843, map). 226 MnDOT, "Ojibwe Sign Translations" (n.d.).
227 Ojibway Research Society of Minnesota (1944, *Report No. 1*, p. 6).

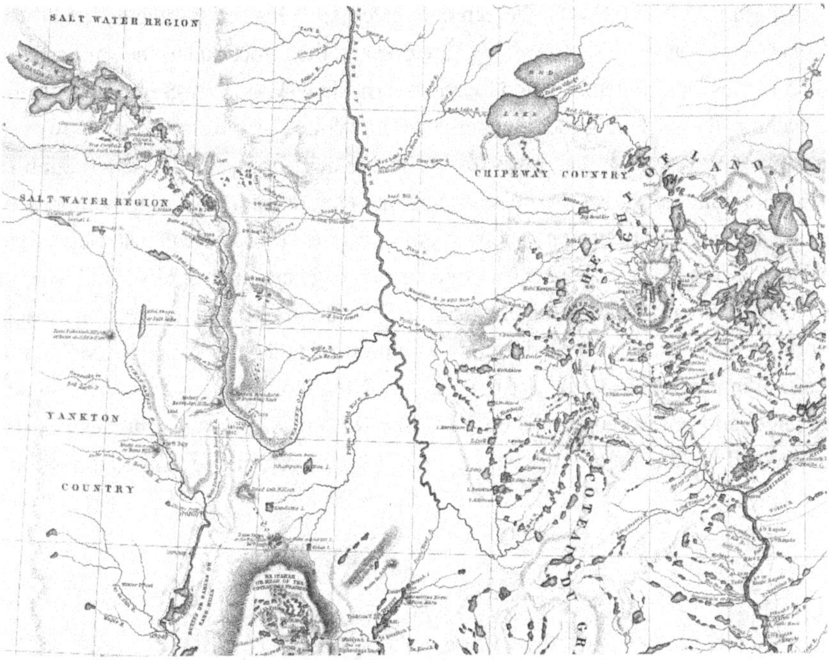

Figure 23 Joseph Nicolas Nicollet's 1843 Map (Detail). Credit: University of Michigan, Clark Library.[228]

Further, in an 1841 US Senate report recounting expeditions during 1836–1839, Nicollet presented the name of a portage and lake – "Ozawewe-satagan" – within an area just south of what would become the White Earth Reservation:

> . . . *Kegwedzissag* pointed out to us a naked bluff on the left bank of the river as the commencement of an important portage, leading to a pretty large lake on the Hauteurs des Terres ["Height of Land"], situated on one of the forks of the Wild Rice river, and whence there is a descent to the Red river of the North. The Indian name of this portage is *Ozawewe-satagan*; which means, according to my apprehension, "to carry baggage from one water to another," and may be significantly rendered in English by "dividing-ridge portage." Here we met with ten canoes filled with Chippeways, coming from lake *Winibigoshish*, who were about undertaking this portage, on their way to the upland lakes to gather wild rice.[229]

Adjacent to the southern end of Tamarac National Wildlife Refuge and directly south of the White Earth Reservation is Height of Land Lake. Its name was recorded in 1944 by the Ojibway Research Society of Minnesota as "Ah-Sha-Way-Way-Se-Tah-Gen-Ning," meaning "Portage from body of water to another"

[228] Nicollet et al. (1843, map). [229] Nicollet (1843, report, p. 60).

(see Figures 24 and 25).[230] We can conclude that "Ozawewe-satagan" and "Ah-Shaw-Way-Way-Se-Tah-Gen-Ning" are one and the same, due to the similarity in their names, their meanings, and locations. Ah-Shaw-Way-Way-Se-Tah-Gen-Ning is technically not within the boundaries of the White Earth Reservation. However, in only being a few miles away from the southern border of the reservation (a 7.6-mile winding drive),[231] the recording and endurance of this toponym demonstrate Ojibwe relationships to this region prior to 1867. Local historian Alvin Wilcox referred to this specific area as a "wigwam metropolis" and site of Ojibwe manoomin harvesting and fishing.[232] With this name referring to a historic portage, with Nicollet recording the migration of Ojibwe ("Chippeways") from Lake Winnibigoshish to the ricing lakes near Height of Land Lake *in 1836* via this portage, and with this lake being a well-known Ojibwe seasonal harvesting site connected to the Otter Tail River, mobility and return are embedded within

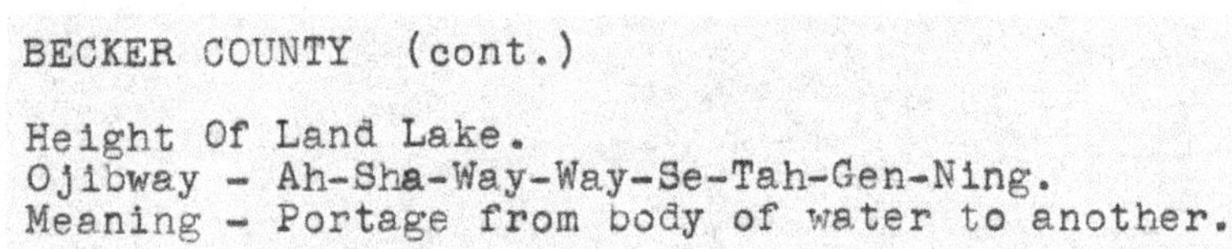

BECKER COUNTY (cont.)

Height Of Land Lake.
Ojibway - Ah-Sha-Way-Way-Se-Tah-Gen-Ning.
Meaning - Portage from body of water to another.

Figure 24 Excerpt from *Report No. 1* by the Ojibway Research Society of Minnesota, April 1, 1944. Includes place names at Gaa-waabaabiganikaag. Image courtesy of the Minnesota Historical Society.[233]

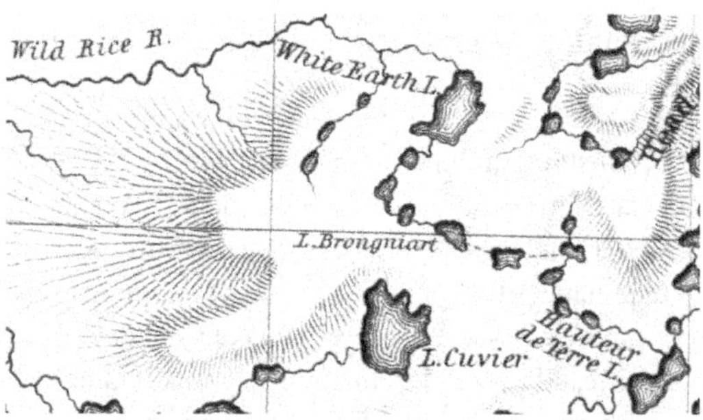

Figure 25 Joseph Nicolas Nicollet's 1843 Map (Detail). Credit: University of Michigan, Clark Library.[234] "Hauteur de Terre L." meaning "Height[s] of Land Lake"[235]

230 Ojibway Research Society of Minnesota (1944, *Report No. 1*, p. 2).
231 Google Maps (Accessed October 16, 2024), https://maps.app.goo.gl/JC7XHSr3MPE5GYKEA.
232 Wilcox (1907, p. 211).
233 Ojibway Research Society of Minnesota (1944, *Report No. 1*, p. 2).
234 Nicollet et al. (1843, map). 235 Nicollet (1843, report, p. 57).

Figures 26, 27, and 28 Neguiquano Sibi/Nigigwanowe-zibi (Otter Tail River) where Ozawewe-satagan /Ah-Sha-Way-Way-Se-Tah-Gen-Ning (Height of Land Lake) meets Rice Lake. Photos by author.

the name of this location and the Ojibwe's intergenerational relationships with this body of water (see Figures 26–28). These maps' depictions of Ojibwe place names, as well as accounts of their meanings documented by nineteenth-century cartographers, demonstrate Anishinaabe people's preexisting relationships to this region prior to the creation of the White Earth Reservation.

Politics of Territorial (Mis)Recognition: Narratives of Convenience and Settler Colonialism

Archived letters, journals, and local histories further confirm that the region of and surrounding Gaa-waabaabiganikaag was defined by Anishinaabe presences, territoriality, and spatial authority before the creation of the White Earth Reservation. In this section, I explicitly assert that the relational structures, property systems, stewardship responsibilities, and seasonal migrations and harvests of Ojibwe people have been constitutive parts of Anishinaabe theorizations and understandings of their own country: Anishinaabe aki. Recalling Brenda Child's and Michael Witgen's writing on "Anishinaabewaki" addressed in the Introduction, long-standing Ojibwe spatial governance and land/water-use protocols have been defined by kinship, obligations, and associated seasonal returns and harvests.[236] Based on their scholarship, the territoriality of Anishinaabe people – especially prior to the reservation period – has been structured around movements, migrations, emergences, returns, obligations, sustainability ethics, and kinship. These elements of Anishinaabe life continue through the practice of reserved treaty rights, which Odawa Elder Frank Ettawageshik refers to as "relationship rights to the land, the water, and all of the beings that we hunt, and fish, and share that world with."[237]

Kyle Whyte addresses how settlers' perceptions, ideologies, and land-use practices have obscured Indigenous presences and environmental relationships. Whyte describes how narrative imaginaries of spatial belonging – "from the doctrine of discovery to the ideologies of 'wilderness'" – emerged within settler colonial societies, serving as rationales for conquest, territorial usurpation, and ecological disruption. Natchee Blu Barnd addresses the function of these narratives within the context of American settler colonialism: "Settlers simply interpreted indigeneity as either lacking proper spatiality or without moral capacity [in stories of 'discovery,' 'terra nullius,' 'virgin landscape,' etc.]."[238] However, as Whyte addresses, these early newcomers did document Indigenous peoples' relationships with their homelands and homewaters, as well as their governing structures and spatial protocols: "In historic accounts of fur traders, clergy, and settlers, they certainly attempted to enclose regions such as Anishinaabewaki into settler concepts of nationhood, savage places, and so on. But in reading those accounts, the colonists nonetheless traveled through

236 Witgen (2011, p. 395); and, Child (2012, pp. 29–30). 237 National Public Radio (2017).
238 Barnd (2017, p. 14).

these regions and recognized the different Indigenous ecologies operative within those places."[239] In this section, records of Ojibwe hunting, fishing, ricing, navigation, kinship obligations, assertions of spatial authority, and expressions of hospitality offer examples of Ojibwe territoriality throughout this region prior to the creation of the White Earth Reservation.

Despite chronicling Native presences and environmental activities, these writings and representations often rely on a perceived tension between Indigenous peoples' claims to place and their patterns of mobility. This rhetorical construction has provided a flawed logical and moral justification for settler colonial territorial accumulation and usurpation. As Anishinaabe people practice(d) seasonal migrations and harvests, their connections and territorial claims to space were (and frequently continue to be) tied to arrivals, departures, and returns. Chantal Norrgard notes how the Anishinaabe concept of [mno] bimaadiziwin (the "good life") has been long pursued by Ojibwe people through their seasonal lifeways referred to as the Anishinaabe seasonal round.[240] These movements and harvests were and are based on the transitions of the seasons and the land/water-use protocols that govern(ed) who had/has access – and who had/has authority to grant access – to respective ricing, hunting, fishing, sugaring, and gathering places.

An example of this constructed tension between rootedness and mobility is found in Alvin Wilcox's *A Pioneer History of Becker County* (1907). While presenting evidence of Ojibwe people's historic environmental relationships, physical presences, and geographic knowledge of Gaa-waabaabiganikaag and its surroundings, Wilcox notes, "The Otter Tail band occupied the country as individuals and families, but I can find no trace of anything resembling the appearance of a village, or permanent headquarters for the habitations of the people anywhere in the county, previous to the settlement of the Indians at White Earth in 1868."[241] With the northern portion of this county overlapping with the White Earth Reservation, Wilcox appears to be denouncing the presence of any preexisting Ojibwe legal claim over the space he describes as "Becker County." However, in correspondence, personal records, interviews, journals, and other archives referenced in Wilcox's history, Ojibwe territorial presence constantly emerges within the pages. Wilcox's inability to recognize harvests and migrations as constitutive of Ojibwe territory and territoriality resonates with other historic dismissals of Indigenous peoples' roots and spatial authority concerning their homewaters and homelands. In this excerpt, perhaps Wilcox demonstrates an unfamiliarity with Anishinaabe governance structures, environmental protocols, and geographic knowledge of this region of

[239] Whyte (2018, pp. 136, 138). [240] Norrgard (2014, pp. 4–5). [241] Wilcox (1907, p. 211).

Anishinaabe aki; however, we may also be reading an individual's judgment of what fails to constitute political/legal presence and what is not legible as a form of nationhood according to Wilcox himself.

Existing scholarship has identified and unpacked the rationales, desires, and (il)logics that have shaped governments' and settlers' claims to lands and waters that have preexisting connections to respective Indigenous peoples and nations. Madeline Whetung describes how the absence of the recognizable symbols of the "fence" (property), "flag" (national identity), "guarded boundaries" (borders restricting mobility), and a "built waterway" (infrastructural transformations of waters and lands) enabled a narrative wherein Nishnaabeg connections to place, modes of territoriality, and land/water-use practices went unobserved by Canadian settlers: " . . . they interpreted this as emptiness, lack of ownership, and attempted to carve themselves into our place. One of the biggest evidences of this is the built waterway on which I paddled."[242] Elder Gidigaa Migizi also spoke of the difficulty that European settlers had in recognizing Nishnaabeg forms of territoriality: "Michi Saagiig Nishnaabeg travelled extensively in our homeland. We moved around according to the seasons. We did not colonize and settle areas like the French and British. They found it difficult to understand how we occupied our territory. They found it difficult to mark us on their maps because we were always moving."[243]

Historic representations of vacant, non-territorialized lands often articulate seasonal migrations as evidence of the absence of Indigenous peoples' and nations' place-based authorities, preexisting relationships, and stewardship roles. Karl Jacoby, writing on the creation of Yellowstone National Park, addresses how seasonal movements of the Shoshone, Crow, Blackfeet, and Bannock were used by early "explorers" of the Yellowstone area to "dismiss[] these natives as transitory nomads." Jacoby examines how Euro-Americans' misrepresentations of Indigenous peoples' relationships enabled the creation of a *convenient* narrative of this region as being without long-standing Native presences or territorial claims, "erasing Indian claims by reclassifying inhabited territory as empty wilderness."[244] Critically, such seasonal migrations and carefully timed harvests demonstrated invaluable environmental and ecological knowledges maintained and practiced by Native peoples across generations.[245]

I posit that failures to recognize Indigenous peoples' land/water-use protocols, governance, stewardship responsibilities, and property systems are expressions of a *politics of (mis)recognition* that remains central to projects of settler colonialism and Indigenous displacement (as addressed by Audra Simpson,[246]

---

[242] Whetung (2016, p. 97). [243] Gidigaa Migizi (2018, p. 30). [244] Jacoby (2003, p. 85).
[245] Jacoby (2003, pp. 85–86). [246] Simpson (2014, pp. 108–109, 134–136).

Glen Coulthard,[247] and Elizabeth Povinelli).[248] I wish to contribute to scholarship on the politics of recognition by bringing forth illustrative examples and theorizations of how Indigenous peoples' and nations' territories have been interpreted and represented as being without preexisting relations prior to the advent of settlement. These narratives may emerge through government agents or affiliates intentionally ignoring or mischaracterizing Indigenous peoples' presences and relationships with their territories and/or through an inability to recognize Native nations' property systems, place-based connections, and/or modes of governance. Despite such failures of recognition, *reports, journals, and maps from the early to mid nineteenth century demonstrate that Gaa-waabaabiganikaag and surrounding waters were places of Ojibwe presence, geographic knowledge, hospitality, and territorial authority.* For the remainder of this section, I present archived records of Ojibwe presences prior to 1867 that were observed throughout Gaa-waabaabiganikaag and the areas that surrounded the forthcoming reservation's boundaries.

Life Cycles and Kinship Obligations

As previously noted, Wilcox describes Ojibwe people's relationships with lands and waters that would later be included within the White Earth Reservation, as well as areas directly south of its forthcoming borders. He identifies the first inhabitants of Becker County as being the "Otter Tail band Pillagers," whose "favorite resort was the Otter Tail River and the country adjacent thereto."[249] The historian depicts a people whose presence was temporary, impermanent. Wilcox largely fails to explicitly recognize the Ojibwe as having any form of preexisting and enduring territorial claim in the region through their presence, their births, their obligations to ancestors, their environmental relationships, their harvests, or their geographic knowledge. However, he does note their place-based relationships, offering us a glimpse into the spatial and territorial lives of the Anishinaabeg of this region prior to 1867.

Ojibwe births and resting places were documented in the area directly south of Gaa-waabaabiganikaag, with these cycles of life taking place decades prior to the creation of the reservation. Wilcox, after stating, "Many of the Pine Point and Otter Tail Indians were born in Becker County," presents the names of a few Ojibwe people born in areas directly south of the forthcoming reservation: John Rock "born at Floyd Lake near Detroit in 1844," Kab-a-mab-hie "born at Rice Lake, three miles south of Frazee, a short time afterwards," and Ma-King "now (1905) about seventy years old . . . [and] was born on the north side of Detroit Lake."[250] In

[247] Coulthard (2014). [248] Povinelli (2002, pp. 55–56, 163). [249] Wilcox (1907, p. 210).
[250] Wilcox (1907, pp. 211–213).

John Schultz's account of his 1860 travels along the "Old Crow Wing Trail" – a route otherwise known as the Woods Trail –, he notes the path's intersection with the Wild Rice River. After crossing this river and traveling south, he observed Ojibwe funerary practices and offerings along Detroit Lake. A portion of the Wild Rice River passes through Gaa-waabaabiganikaag, with Detroit Lake being directly south of what would become the White Earth Reservation. During his travels, Schultz observed Ojibwe presence through ceremonial activities and care of ancestors at Detroit Lake.[251]

In Wilcox's and Schultz's accounts, Ojibwe individuals "occupied" the area,[252] were born there, and engaged in funerary practices directly south of the forthcoming borders of the White Earth Reservation. Jurisdiction over the noted areas of Detroit Lake and Floyd Lake would be asserted by Becker County in 1871 with its initial organization and the creation of a board of county commissioners.[253] While the county was created by the legislature of Minnesota in 1858, according to Wilcox's history, "There were, however, no white people living in the county for ten years afterwards."[254] Taken together, these records demonstrate preexisting Ojibwe presence, ceremonial life, birth, and death within this region. These archives provide evidence that these were Ojibwe homelands and homewaters directly south of Gaa-waabaabiganikaag in the decades prior to the creation of the White Earth Reservation.

Harvests and Returns

Ojibwe hunting, fishing, and ricing activities were documented within the forthcoming boundaries of White Earth and in the region south of the reservation prior to Ojibwe relocations to the reservation in 1868. For certain Anishinaabe people such as Paul Beaulieu, these migrations of the late 1860s were returns rather than initial arrivals. In a letter to Wilcox, Paul's nephew Gus Beaulieu describes an Ojibwe winter hunt that took place at Gaa-waabaabiganikaag, roughly twenty years prior to the creation of the reservation. Paul Beaulieu was involved in the hunt, as well as Ojibwe parties traveling from Sandy Lake and Red Lake that gathered around White Earth Lake in February 1848. Paul's obituary published in the *Detroit Record* provides important information about his life, noting that he "was born at Mackinac in 1820," "was of French and Indian descent," "took an active part . . . in all matters relating to the Chippewa Indians," and "was reputed to be the most fluent interpreter of the Chippewa dialect that the nation ever produced."[255] Gus[256] provided a summary of events that was printed in Wilcox's

[251] Schultz (1894, pp. 4, 21). [252] Wilcox (1907, p. 211). [253] Wilcox (1907, p. 275).
[254] Wilcox (1907, p. 9). [255] Wilcox (1907, p. 258).
[256] Minnesota Historical Society, "The Progress" (n.d.); and, Minnesota Historical Society, "The Tomahawk" (n.d.).

1907 history, which were previously shared by "Canadian voyageur" Jaques Courrier and Joseph Jourdan, "one of the oldest members on this reservation." Gus includes geographic references to areas within the forthcoming boundaries of the reservation, with the sites of this hunt being "White Earth Lake and vicinity," as well as referencing his father Clement Beaulieu's work for the American Fur Company in "Chippewa country." This letter demonstrates that the 1848 hunt by Ojibwe people took place on lands that would become the White Earth Reservation, while including mention of the area that would become the White Earth agency.[257]

In his local history, Wilcox describes seasonal harvests at Height of Land Lake and surrounding areas, with the Otter Tail River running through this region. He presents evidence of Ojibwe fishing and wild ricing in this area and around "Round Lake on the White Earth Reservation" and Shell Lake:[258]

> There were, however, occasional temporary gatherings, and the outlet of Height of Land Lake was the most frequent place of rendezvous . . . there had been a fish trap built across the Otter Tail River, a short distance below the outlet, a long time ago, where fish could be secured in abundance at all seasons of the year. At the upper end of Height of Land Lake and the two lakes first above mentioned were the most extensive and valuable wild rice beds in the whole region of country: all of which made the vicinity of Height of Land Lake a kind of wigwam metropolis for the Otter Tail Indians on various occasions.[259]

Wilcox dismisses these harvests as evidence of Ojibwe territorial claims and possession, asserting that they were "occasional temporary gatherings," as well as previously noting the absence of any Ojibwe "village, or permanent head-quarters" prior to the creation of the White Earth Reservation.[260] I argue that this is a narrative of convenience, insofar as Ojibwe presence in the region that would later be claimed by Becker County – both within and directly south of White Earth – is represented as being based on "temporary" residence, harvests, and gatherings, rather than seasonal cycles of returns and departures that constituted the basis of the Ojibwe seasonal round. Wilcox's descriptions of spaces marked by Ojibwe presence but not spatial authority prior to 1867 fail to recognize how Ojibwe property and territorial claims were often intertwined

257 Beaulieu (1907, pp. 54–55).

258 Note: Wilcox (1907) writes, "At the upper end of Height of Land Lake and the two lakes first above mentioned were the most extensive and valuable wild rice beds in the whole region of country" (p. 211). On that same page, he mentions "Round Lake on the White Earth Reservation," "Shell Lake," and "Detroit Lake" in that order, being the first mentions of lakes in Chapter XIII (aside from Height of Land Lake which was already explicitly named by Wilcox) (p. 211).

259 Wilcox (1907, p. 211). 260 Wilcox (1907, p. 211).

with the seasonal round, wherein cyclical migrations, environmental knowledge, sustainable harvests, stewardship obligations, and property rights constituted Anishinaabe territory and forms of territoriality.

Locating the White Earth Reservation

Ojibwe geographic knowledge of their country between the Red River and the Mississippi proved critical for the well-being of non-Native traders and government officials attempting to move throughout this area. The very location of the White Earth Reservation was recollected by Joseph Wakefield as being based on an 1862 trip he took with Indian agent Edwin Clark, when they depended on Otter Tail Ojibwe to safely navigate their travels from Detroit Lake to Clearwater to issue payments to the "Otter Tail, Pembina and Red Lake [Ojibwe] Indians." On his and Clark's reliance on the Ojibwe, Wakefield wrote:

> We followed the old Red River Trail, and camped at Detroit Lake on our way out . . . It was a wild trip. The Sioux were all over the country, and were very hostile: it being soon after the beginning of the terrible massacre in southern Minnesota [a reference to the U.S.-Dakota War]. The Otter Tail Indians escorted us through to the Clearwater.[261]

It is not clear if Wakefield and Clark were dependent on the Ojibwe solely for protection or also for their geographic knowledge; however, we can confirm that they relied on Anishinaabe people for safe travels as they traversed to and through the land of the white clay in 1862. On this trip facilitated by Ojibwe navigators, Wakefield and Clark compared Gaa-waabaabiganikaag to "the Garden of Eden" and noted it as an ideal place for a reservation, which they communicated to US government officials.[262]

Wakefield's discussion of his work preparing the reservation for the Ojibwe in 1868 (tilling soil for agriculture and harvesting timber for constructing "agency buildings") includes a reference to Paul Beaulieu (Ojibwe/French)[263] as being "the leader of the party . . . [being] employed by the government as farmer and surveyor."[264] In Julia Ann Warren Spears' "History of White Earth" (included in Wilcox's history), Paul Beaulieu is described as "one of the first settlers, and was government farmer during the first two years of the settlement of White Earth Reservation. He ploughed and made the first garden in White Earth."[265] Paul Beaulieu's mention among the first recorded peoples of White Earth and Becker County is noteworthy for a variety of reasons. According to Wakefield, the federal government selected Beaulieu as leading one of the first government work parties to White Earth in April 1868 "because he knew better

[261] Wakefield (1906, pp. 240–241). [262] Wakefield (1906, pp. 240–241).
[263] Wilcox (1907, p. 258). [264] Wakefield (1906, pp. 240–241). [265] Spears (1907, p. 256).

how to manage the fording of the rivers," with Beaulieu serving as a government "farmer and surveyor."[266] Here, Ojibwe geographic knowledge and navigational prowess were central for moving to and through Gaa-waabaabiganikaag. While Beaulieu was often referred to as the founder and first resident of the White Earth Reservation in Spears and Wilcox's histories, his life trajectory demonstrated both mobility and place-based connections throughout Anishinaabe aki. As a child, Paul Beaulieu was originally from Mackinac,[267] had matrilineal Ojibwe and patrilineal French ancestry, attended the Mackinaw Mission School, and had a father who was a trader based in the western Great Lakes region.[268] Two decades after the bison hunt surrounding White Earth Lake, Paul Beaulieu was supporting the relocation of Ojibwe people to the White Earth Reservation. For Beaulieu, the 1868 Ojibwe "settlement" of White Earth would be a geographic return, rather than initial arrival.

Navigation, Hospitality, Protection, and Authority: Ojibwe Influence throughout the Woods Trail

The creation and use of the Woods Trail demonstrates preexisting Ojibwe geographic knowledge throughout its route. This wagon road created in 1844[269] (or possibly earlier)[270] was utilized by Red River traders transporting goods. The trail passed through portions of Gaa-waabaabiganikaag, the area that would become known as the White Earth Reservation. In Wilcox's history of Becker County, he notes that already present trails passing through Becker County were observed by early Euro-American settlers. We can deduce that these paths – referred to as the "old Red River Road" by Wilcox – were part of the Woods Trail (also known as the "Crow Wing Trail").[271] Wilcox offers the following geographic description of the path's course through Gaa-waabaabiganikaag: "[the road] then crossed the Buffalo River at the old bridge, and thence in a northerly direction across the White Earth Reservation to Pembina."[272] The trail's name references its route through heavily forested

266 Wakefield (1906, p. 240). 267 Wilcox (1907, p. 258). 268 De Rosa (2010, p. 712).

269 Gilman et al. (1979, p. 9).

270 Wilcox (1907, pp. 217–218). Note: Wilcox reproduces a letter by the "Hon. R. M. Probsfield of Moorhead" when trying to date the origin of the road, who wrote, "I do not know when the old road was first established, but was told by Norman W. Kittson that he used that trail in the late thirties, say between 1837 and 1840, on his way to and from Prairie Du Chien, Wisconsin and Pembina and Ft. Gar[r]y, now Winnipeg" (p. 218). Wilcox also states, "My opinion is that the road was opened up soon after the dividing line was agreed upon by the Sioux and Chippewas between their respective territories, which was on the 19th of August, 1825 [Treaty of Prairie du Chien]" (p. 217).

271 Gilman et al. (1979, pp. 12, 55).

272 Wilcox (1907, p. 217); and, Gilman et al. (1979, pp. 55–68, see map on p. 61).

areas between Crow Wing and Detroit Lake.[273] Elaborating on this road's significance for those who traversed it, Wilcox writes,

> The only road connecting the settlements of Pembina on the lower Red River and Fort Snelling and other points on the Mississippi lower down, before that time, passed through ... the heart of the Sioux country, whereas a road through by the new route would pass through a section of country owned altogether by the Chippewas, and would be considered much safer ...[274]

The construction of the Woods Trail was of great significance for traders and wagon drivers, as its route through Ojibwe country helped ensure their safety from Dakota interference in their travels.[275]

In *The Red River Trails*, Rhoda Gilman, Carolyn Gilman, and Deborah Stultz (hereafter "Gilman et al.") effectively synthesize primary sources to chronicle the creation and use of the Woods Trail, while also including maps depicting the trail moving through Gaa-waabaabiganikaag *prior to* the reservation's creation. These scholars address how an 1872 survey identified the trail and a connecting road as passing through towns and near waters within the White Earth Reservation, including Mahnomen, Waubun, White Earth, Wild Rice River, and Elbow Lake.[276] Gilman et al. state the Woods Trail initially emerged in October and November of 1844, on a trip undertaken by traders including Peter Garrioch (Scottish-Cree ancestry).[277] Garrioch's journal illustrates how Ojibwe people's navigational prowess, geographic knowledge, and hospitality within Anishinaabe territory were central to the initial creation and navigation of the trail. In Garrioch's 1844 account of creating the trail to avoid passing through Dakota territory, he describes great difficulty in cutting a path through the forested regions along the Crow Wing River. Their luck changed on October 13 when a "man of the Chipeways [Ojibwe]" named Nine Fingers agreed to serve as their guide for the stretch to Otter Tail Lake.[278] With "provisions almost entirely out," Nine Fingers provided the traders five ducks and a bear on October 19.[279] A large camp of friendly Anishinaabe people – "a dozen tents of the pillagers" – were at Otter Tail Lake when Garrioch and the traders arrived on October 22. According to Garrioch, these Pillager Ojibwe "evinced the greatest satisfaction in our passing through their country and assured us that both we and our property would be treated with the greatest civility ..."[280] Garrioch notes that on October 23, "Being entirely out of provisions ... I purchased for myself and man [*sic*] 2 bushels rice, about 200

[273] Gilman et al. (1979, p. 55). [274] Wilcox (1907, pp. 217–218).
[275] Schultz (1894, p. 12); and, Garrioch (1844, p. 23). [276] Gilman et al. (1979, p. 62).
[277] Gilman et al. (1979, p. 9). [278] Garrioch (1844, pp. 27, 30–31)
[279] Garrioch (1844, p. 28). [280] Garrioch (1844, p. 28).

dryed [*sic*] fish, 40 fresh, and a bag of pounded fish" at Otter Tail Lake.[281] Ojibwe hospitality and economic activity was necessary for the survival and well-being of the Red River traders navigating an unfamiliar terrain with scarce supplies.[282]

Nine Fingers' geographic expertise and hunting skills were critical to the development of portions of the Woods Trail. The Anishinaabe guide continued assisting Garrioch and his crew past Otter Tail Lake, facilitating their movement north in creating the trail. On November 5, Garrioch and his party exited the dense woodlands, with the landscape transitioning into navigable prairie.[283] Nine Fingers departed the traders on November 6, allowing us to deduce that the Pillager Ojibwe navigator was instrumental in facilitating Garrioch and company's creation of a difficult and sizeable stretch of the Woods Trail.[284] The portion of the Woods Trail passing through Gaa-waabaabiganikaag would be traveled in a matter of days, with Garrioch, his company, and their carts crossing the Rice River on the 10th and arriving to the "river of Sandy hills" on November 13.[285] Arriving at the Wild Rice River merely days after Nine Fingers' departure demonstrates their successful reliance on Anishinaabe geographic knowledge through extremely challenging terrain to reach this point.

Little is conveyed about this Ojibwe guide in Garrioch's diary despite Nine Fingers' significant contributions to the Woods Trail's creation. Garrioch's descriptions of Nine Fingers are brief and reductive: "a man of the Chipeways" (October 13) and "our Guide, an untutored savage" (October 19). Three years after helping Garrioch and company navigate and construct this portion of the Woods Trail, Nine Fingers' x-mark would be included within an August 21, 1847, treaty between the Pillager Band of Chippewa and the United States: "Chang a so ning, or nine fingers, 3d Head man his x mark."[286] Garrioch's journal entries for the period when his company was guided and nourished by Nine Fingers (October 13–November 6, 1844) entirely fail to account for the governing role(s) and leadership status of this Ojibwe person among the Otter Tail Pillagers.[287] Being one of nine representatives of the Pillager Ojibwe named signatory to this agreement, we can deduce that Nine Fingers' role within the governance of his nation was significant. An 1858 report by missionaries further confirms Chang-a-so-ning's position as a leader.[288] While it is not clear if Garrioch was unaware of Chang-a-so-ning's political standing

281 Garrioch (1844, pp. 28–29).
282 Gilman et al. (1979, p. 9); and, Garrioch (1844, pp. 27–29).
283 Garrioch (1844, pp. 30–31); and, Gilman et al. (1979, pp. 9–10).
284 Garrioch (1844, pp. 30, 31).
285 Garrioch (1844, pp. 31–32).
286 "Ratified Indian Treaty 251: Chippewa (Pillager Band) – Leech Lake, August 21, 1847" (1847).
287 Garrioch (1844, pp. 27–31).
288 Kemper et al. (1858, pp. 800–804).

within his nation, if Garrioch merely failed to record these details in his journals, or if Nine Fingers was not yet considered an ogimaa of the Otter Tail Pillager Ojibwe in 1844, knowledge of his leadership adds critical context to how we interpret his role and intentions in providing navigation and sustenance during Red River traders' first passage along the Woods Trail. In guiding Garrioch and his crew through this wooded terrain, Nine Fingers was perhaps not only offering geographic guidance and hunted foods for a $12 fee; he may have been acting diplomatically while surveilling the movements, migrations, and intentions of those passing through Ojibwe country.

Starving near the end of their 1844 journey, Garrioch and his companions came upon "a village of Red lake Indians who had plenty of fresh and dried meat" on November 26. Describing these Anishinaabeg as "hospitable and kind," Garrioch detailed how Red Lake Ojibwe people provided them food, "provisions for the rest of [their] journey," and directions for crossing the Red River.[289] Garrioch's journal demonstrates that a large portion of the Woods Trail was created as a result of the critical geographic knowledge of Ojibwe people from the Pillager and Red Lake Bands. These entries evidence preexisting Anishinaabe knowledge of the geography of their country and how to successfully traverse their territory. Garrioch's journal illustrates that the creation of the Woods Trail in 1844 was largely a story of Ojibwe presence, navigation, authority, and hospitality[290] within Anishinaabe aki.

Anishinaabe people also directly articulated that the Woods Trail passed through Ojibwe country. Recalling that the impetus for the Woods Trail's construction was a desire to travel "safer" through Ojibwe territories – rather than those of the Dakota – the pathway and its surroundings were at least implicitly acknowledged by Red River traders including Garrioch as being located within Anishinaabe aki.[291] Beginning in 1854, the Middle Trail and Woods Trail became the most traveled routes associated with the Red River fur and commercial trade.[292] Traversing the trail were the infamously squeaky wooden wheels[293] of Red River carts, being pushed by Indian ponies or oxen (as described in Hind's 1857 and Schultz's 1860 accounts).[294] Ojibwe responses to the increasing flow of traders within their country demonstrated a recognition of this pathway as firmly within their territory. On October 29, 1846, two Ojibwe hunters met Robert Clouston, a Hudson's Bay Company clerk, where the Woods Trail met the Buffalo River. After Clouston refused to trade with the Ojibwe, they asserted, "that for several years they had allowed

[289] Garrioch (1844, p. 36); and, Gilman et al. (1979, p. 10). [290] Gilman et al. (1979, p. 10).
[291] Garrioch (1844, p. 23). [292] Gilman et al. (1979, p. 16). [293] Gilman et al. (1979, p. 16).
[294] Hind (1860, pp. 253–264); and, Schultz (1894, pp. 12–22).

Red River people to pass through their lands, frightening away the wild animals and had not received even a mouthful of provisions from them . . . [and] vowed that in the future they would levy blackmail [i.e., a fee] on all passers by."[295] The threat of a toll for traversing the trail demonstrates that these two hunters understood its route as passing through Ojibwe territory which was subject to Anishinaabe jurisdiction and regulation. On such tensions concerning spatial authority, Gilman et al. write, "*No agreement had ever been sought or given for the passage of cart trains through the lands of the Dakota or the Ojibwe.*"[296] The Ojibwe hunters' threat of fining a toll for traders to compensate for interrupting their hunting can be understood as occurring in a context of ecological disruption and trespass. In this 1846 interaction, Ojibwe people were asserting their sovereignty, jurisdiction, and authority to regulate trade within their homelands. Created prior to the establishment of the White Earth Reservation, the Woods Trail was a route within Ojibwe Country, a pathway created through Anishinaabe navigational prowess, a site of hospitality extended by Anishinaabe people, and a place where Ojibwe spatial authority was articulated.

Conclusion: A Reservation within Anishinaabe Aki

The archives addressed in this section communicate Gaa-waabaabiganikaag as a place marked by Ojibwe presence, places names, geographic knowledge, seasonal harvests and returns, and navigational prowess prior to the creation of the White Earth Reservation in 1867. With Red River merchants relying on the Woods Trail to transport furs and goods safely throughout "Chippewa country" beginning in 1844, this area was recognized as a place of Ojibwe authority and hospitality in the journals and correspondence of traders. In this section, three regions and scales of Anishinaabe aki (i.e., Anishinaabe territory) have been addressed: the waters and lands that would later be within the White Earth Reservation; the areas immediately surrounding the forthcoming reservation's boundaries (e.g., Detroit Lake and Height of Land Lake); and the larger area between the Mississippi River and Red River of the North understood as under Ojibwe control (as described in the 1825 Treaty of Prairie du Chien). However, Anishinaabe territory extended far beyond the boundaries of Gaa-waabaabiganikaag, beyond the immediate surroundings of the forthcoming reservation, and even beyond these two great rivers. Within the extensive spatial expanse of Anishinaabe aki throughout the

[295] Clouston (1846, pp. 1, 52); and, Gilman et al. (1979, p. 10).

[296] Gilman et al. (1979, p. 23, emphasis mine).

Great Lakes region and Turtle Island prior to 1867, the Land of White Clay and its immediate surroundings were places where Ojibwe people practiced seasonal ricing, fishing, and hunting, offered guidance and security for traders and government officials, and had preexisting place names for bodies of water in Anishinaabemowin. As evidenced in this section, the roots of Ojibwe people at Gaa-waabaabiganikaag predate the creation of the White Earth Reservation.

Conclusion: "It Sits in Your Spirit and It Starts Taking Root Again": Mapping the Endurance of Ojibwe Geographic Knowledge and Relationships

In crafting this Element, I have addressed how bilingual road signs featuring Ojibwe place names at White Earth have been informed by efforts to preserve and revitalize knowledge of these toponyms. These names for bodies of water at Gaa-waabaabiganikaag have been used and recognized by generations of Ojibwe people, were shared by the Anishinaabe informants of Gilfillan and Watrin, were recorded in the collaborative reports of the Ojibway-Dakota Research Society, and, most recently, were made publicly visible on the roads of Gaa-waabaabiganikaag through the efforts of the White Earth Nation cultural committee. When passing these sheet aluminum markers while driving throughout the White Earth Reservation, Anishinaabemowin and English place names are represented. However, beneath the Anishinaabemowin toponyms are Ojibwe histories and memories of these waters, of geographic knowledge transmission and preservation across generations, and decisions on how, why, and where these names should be publicly recorded and represented. These signs featuring Anishinaabemowin demonstrate a desire for Ojibwe geographic knowledge to be publicly witnessed within the boundaries of Gaa-waabaabiganikaag. The Anishinaabemowin toponyms depicted on road signs are now part of the constitution of Ojibwe spatial belonging and environmental connection within the White Earth Reservation. In this conclusion, I illustrate the endurance of place-based relationships throughout Gaa-waabaabiganikaag while contextualizing these connections through a focus on intergenerational geographic knowledge. The continuation of seasonal hunting, fishing, ricing, and gathering across generations of White Earth Ojibwe families – as articulated in ethnographic interviews – demonstrates how Anishinaabe people have centered inherited knowledges of place by retaining and renewing specific spatial connections throughout the White Earth Reservation.

Family Stories and Intergenerational Geographic Connections

Beyond the presence of Anishinaabemowin toponym road signs, the Ojibwe of and from the White Earth Reservation have long, intergenerational histories of belonging to specific places throughout Gaa-waabaabiganikaag. Interviews conducted with White Earth Anishinaabeg in recent years demonstrate the endurance of these spatial bonds into the present, with Ojibwe people describing familial connections to specific seasonal gathering, hunting, ricing, and fishing spots. The lives, movements, harvests, and presences of these Anishinaabe people persist despite legacies of imposed territorial, environmental, ecological, jurisdictional, and linguistic displacements. This demonstrates Ojibwe survivance and ongoing relationships to sites of familial and relational significance. I wish to share a few stories from ethnographic interviews wherein Ojibwe people of White Earth described their families' connections to place. These relationships are associated with seasonal activities of gathering, ricing, fishing, and hunting. While these stories are not about toponyms, they testify to the importance of specific locales and bodies of water for themselves, their families, and/or the wider White Earth Anishinaabe community. These stories demonstrate the endurance of inherited geographic knowledge through seasonal returns and spatial belonging in the present.

During a July 2017 interview, Megan Bakken – the current Land Office Manager and former Realty Leasing Coordinator for White Earth – discussed how she inherited knowledge of gathering locations from her family. In the following set of excerpts, Megan described what the inheritance of place can consist of for White Earth families:

> We always frequent the same areas. When we pick mushrooms in the spring, we go to the same spot. Like twenty other people also go to the same spot, so it's first-come, first-serve. It's just something we do . . . Growing up, I always remember going out picking asparagus and mushrooms and then, about this time of year, we'd go up to [lake name redacted] and pick blueberries. We've always done chokecherries, well we did when I was younger. And now, where I am, I make sure I have a lot of plants. We do a lot of canning, stuff at home. So we do a lot of that . . .[297]

When I asked Megan if those locations for gathering mushrooms, chokecherries, and blueberries were passed down through her family, she shared, "Yeah, I think we've always gone to the same old areas."[298] After conveying how more and more people are gathering foods from the shared harvesting sites she knew of through her family, Megan described the process of looking for new locations by traversing the reservation and being attentive of those foods that emerge in different areas: "Now, with so many people going to the same areas, we've looked at expanding . . . We drive down different roads and look at different areas and just try to look at the vegetation and guess."[299] Even if attempts to locate new spaces for foraging are unsuccessful, the process of scouting new gathering spots teaches her children how to develop this analytical skill for

[297] "Interview with Megan Bakken," interview conducted by Elan Pochedley, White Earth Reservation, July 20, 2017.

[298] "Interview with Megan Bakken," interview conducted by Elan Pochedley, White Earth Reservation, July 20, 2017.

[299] "Interview with Megan Bakken," interview conducted by Elan Pochedley, White Earth Reservation, July 20, 2017.

those moments when their family grounds cannot support them: "Sometimes we get lucky, sometimes we don't. More often not. But it's teaching the little kids gathering, too."[300] When I asked if she thought it was common for families who've grown up at White Earth to pass along that geographic knowledge and connections to gathering places to their descendants, Megan replied:

> I think so . . . when I think about it, I can relate it to mushrooms. 'Cause people are always [saying] "Well, I'm going out to my spot to pick mushrooms," and it's like a super-secret thing. I've always picked them out here all my life, so I know where they grow. We've gotten to a point where the kids kind of know where they grow now. But it's always in our spot . . . Even when we were trying to find new spots, just driving around in different areas, I felt out of place. It's still on the reservation, but it just felt weird. I think a lot of people feel that way, or at least I do. And I think my family . . . my older brother, he was a little different though. He didn't work, so he'd do a lot of that: he'd fish, rice, leech. He could pretty much go anywhere. But he still kept to some of the same areas too. So I think that feeling of home is there.[301]

Will Bement, the current Fisheries Manager and former Water Resources Manager for White Earth, shared the story of how his relationships to place within the reservation are rooted in his parents' and grandparents' connections to the waters of Gaa-waabaabiganikaag. He told me: "Ever since I was little, my grandparents, my parents basically lived outside. That's what we did. You know, you were always hunting, you were leeching, you were ricing . . . I even remember going darkhouse spearing with my dad . . . I was just little . . . I remember things like that. Just always being an outdoors family."[302] Will described how, when he was harvesting manoomin with his grandma, she would communicate significant protocols and teachings concerning the sustainable and respectful harvesting of wild rice:

> But when we were out, we'd visit about a lot of different things. You know, again, this is coming back, "When you're doing it, you don't want to knock the head off. This is how you make sure you know when it's ripe." She just . . . you just learn over time by visiting with her. She wasn't preaching to us or anything, you'd just talk to her and you'd pick up on things like that.[303]

300 "Interview with Megan Bakken," interview conducted by Elan Pochedley, White Earth Reservation, July 20, 2017.

301 "Interview with Megan Bakken," interview conducted by Elan Pochedley, White Earth Reservation, July 20, 2017.

302 "Interview with Will Bement," interview conducted by Elan Pochedley, White Earth Reservation, August 3, 2017.

303 "Interview with Will Bement," interview conducted by Elan Pochedley, White Earth Reservation, August 3, 2017.

By including Will in their fishing and manoomin harvesting, his parents and grandparents continued intergenerational and familial connections to waters within and surrounding the reservation. These excerpts demonstrate that, while recorded Ojibwe place names generally illustrate Anishinaabe people's relationships to the lakes and rivers of the reservation, stories of enduring bonds to place permeate the lived experiences and inherited knowledges of the White Earth Ojibwe.

During a July 2017 interview, Katherine – the former Director of the White Earth Land Office – discussed how her role in protecting the reservation lands and resources had been passed down from her grandmother and mother, with the latter leading the White Earth Land Office for nearly twenty years:

> I guess for me and my family, we have a lot of medicine connections. There's a lot of medicinal uses in our family history . . . My grandma used to go pick medicine with other elder women and help them . . . different stuff like that. Just knowing that medicine is on the ground and growing, that it's coming forth, that you want to preserve it. You want to know it will be there in the future, and getting back into the use of them, and not so reliant on the Government's medical system. God put the herbs of the field for our healing. Getting our health back into the place our body was created for. So that's my connection.[304]

For Katherine, there is a direct relation between protecting the environments and other-than-human life, understanding medicines, observing the language, and finding a sense of home after legacies of dispossession and mistreatment. On the blossoming visual presence of Anishinaabemowin throughout White Earth, she articulates the following: "Where now, we're starting to see it come back. And you're seeing it in the signs. You're seeing it on walls and on pictures and posters and ads. *It just kind of sits in your spirit and it starts taking root again.* I think that's gonna be a positive in the future as we move forward with it."[305]

Merlin – the Director of the White Earth Cultural Division – also addressed inheriting familial stories and relationships to specific hunting and ricing locations. He described how his family migrated between Minneapolis and the White Earth Reservation throughout his childhood. In our conversation, he discussed how, through his parents and grandparents, he has maintained place-based connections to specific waters and lands at Gaa-waabaabiganikaag during his life. Detailing his family's seasonal presences on the reservation, Merlin

[304] "Interview with Katherine Warren," interview conducted by Elan Pochedley, White Earth Reservation, July 19, 2017. Includes additions submitted on February 6, 2025.

[305] "Interview with Katherine Warren," interview conducted by Elan Pochedley, White Earth Reservation, July 19, 2017 (emphasis mine).

shared: " . . . then in the wintertime, we'd come back up too. But we'd always come up in the summertime . . . So we'd always come up for deer hunting, duck hunting, and ricing. So a lot of Indians that live in Minneapolis, they do come back and forth. And so that's how they keep their connection up here with the seasonal hunting . . ."[306] Merlin detailed how place-based connections across generations of his family are contained, retained, and transferred through their stories of hunting on Gaa-waabaabiganikaag:

> Yeah, you know you follow your parents. We all follow our parents and our grandparents. So I know when we would come back up . . . my grandpa and grandma grew up here their whole lives and moved down to the cities when they got a little bit older. So whenever I come back up here, I think of my parents and my grandparents. We would go deer hunting in certain spots where my grandpa would go or my dad would go. My dad actually had a lot of old stories of hunting, hunting stories over there in Naytahwaush: a lot of old places over there where they would kill a lot of deer and a lot of ducks and partridges and so forth. It becomes intergenerational I guess, the stories that would be shared by my parents and my grandparents and so forth. That's kind of how you have that connection. That connection to the land is through the stories, individual family stories and there is a lot of stories that my dad told me that were true that happened in Naytahwaush over there, 'cause my grandpa and grandma and my dad, that was their home.[307]

With Merlin and his family moving between Minneapolis and Gaa-waabaabiganikaag in his youth, they were traveling between the two homes of many members of the Ojibway-Dakota Research Society, as addressed in Section 3. The creation of that research society was made possible through Ojibwe people's movements between the White Earth Reservation and the Twin Cities. While Merlin and his family would return to White Earth for seasonal hunts and wild ricing, research society members from White Earth (including co-founders William Madison and Joseph Fairbanks)[308] would discuss the Ojibwe names for lakes and rivers throughout Gaa-waabaabiganikaag and Anishinaabe aki while living in the Twin Cities. In their own respective ways, these migrations were critical to the enduring practice, enactment, memory, and preservation of Ojibwe geographic knowledge and place-based connections concerning the waters of Gaa-waabaabiganikaag.

---

306 "Interview with Merlin," interview conducted by Elan Pochedley, White Earth Reservation, August 2, 2017.

307 "Interview with Merlin," interview conducted by Elan Pochedley, White Earth Reservation, August 2, 2017.

308 Ojibway-Dakota Research Society of Minnesota (1963, pp. 5–6); and, Ojibway-Dakota Research Society of Minnesota (1945, *Report No. 2*, p. 12).

Ancestral Names and Intergenerational Knowledge throughout Anishinaabe Aki

These Ojibwe toponym markers at White Earth do not transcend the borders of the reservation into the homewaters and homelands of Ojibwe people: their physical presence is restricted to within the reservation. In being spatially confined in this way, their locations do not trouble or contest the settler colonial logics of enclosure that animated the creation of reservations throughout the nineteenth century, including at White Earth.[309] In this sense, they differ from recent public signage initiatives by the Ogimaa Mikana Project and the Grand Portage Band of Lake Superior Chippewa, whose markers stretch throughout Anishinaabe aki, beyond reservation borders.[310] However, the White Earth Nation and the cultural committee were pushing against other forms of enclosure that have historically and contemporarily impacted Anishinaabe life at Gaa-waabaabiganikaag. With the White Earth Reservation being a site of intense dispossession, these signs offer a powerful reminder that Gaa-waabaabiganikaag is a space marked by Ojibwe presence, belonging, history, and knowledge. With Anishinaabemowin being previously prohibited at residential, mission, and day schools – where Ojibwe youth's public use of their own language historically resulted in physical and psychological violence –,[311] these signs demonstrate the endurance of Anishinaabemowin despite the protracted impacts of these institutions on Ojibwe language fluency. These markers were also installed during the contemporary period when Ojibwe language revitalization efforts are a critical priority of White Earth and other Anishinaabe nations. With these place names being located by Sonny McDougall and Mary Otto in a 1963 article, the WEN cultural committee brought these archived toponyms into the visual fields and consciousnesses of Ojibwe people by introducing visible representations of these names next to respective bodies of water at White Earth (see Figure 29). In these place names moving from archives in the Twin Cities to the road signs of Gaa-waabaabiganikaag, the cultural committee was also avoiding constructed temporal enclosures and associations of archives with the past and public signage with the present. The visual emergence of Ojibwe place names indicates that these toponyms continue to hold modern significance while having deep historical roots. While knowledge of these toponyms for lakes and a river may have been temporarily suppressed, the work of generations of Ojibwe people to preserve these names has culminated in the emergence of public signage, demonstrating

[309] U.S. Office of Indian Affairs (1867, p. 24); White Earth Reservation Curriculum Committee et al. (1989, pp. 25–26); and, Meyer (1999).

[310] Note: Please see the reference section for sources and news stories addressing public signs by the Ogimaa Mikana Project and the Grand Portage Band of Lake Superior Chippewa.

[311] Vannote and Pratt (1999, p. 74).

Figure 29 Bemijigamaasing sign. Photo by author.

the endurance of Anishinaabe geographic knowledge in respect to the waters of Gaa-waabaabiganikaag.

These signs are present at Gaa-waabaabiganikaag largely due to the efforts of the Ojibway-Dakota Research Society during the 1940s and 1950s. Recording, preserving, and sharing these place names left traces for upcoming generations of Ojibwe people to follow, embodying Heid Erdrich's theorization of name' and Ojibwe literary ancestors.[312] That research group, in their time, had documented their own knowledge while also reflecting on earlier reports focusing on Ojibwe toponyms, which were themselves rooted in Ojibwe people sharing their geographic knowledge with Joseph Gilfillan and Benno Watrin. This pattern continues going further back, with Joseph Nicollet's 1843 map being informed by Ojibwe guides Chagobay, Kégouédgikâ/Kegwedzissag, and Brunia, with whom he traveled throughout the Mississippi headwaters region in 1836.[313] These stories of toponymic transmission and preservation are tied to textual recordings

[312] Erdrich (2013, p. 14).

[313] Nicollet (1836/1970, pp. 34, 46, 85–86, 88, 90, 127); Nicollet (1843, report, p. 60); Northern Community Radio – KAXE & KBXE, "Our History: The Journey of Chagobay and Brunia – Ten-part series," Part 7 (2012); and, Northern Community Radio – KAXE & KBXE, "Our History: The Journey of Chagobay and Brunia – Ten-part series," Part 10 (2012).

of Ojibwe people's geographic knowledge; I do not attend to the likely abundant stories of Anishinaabe people sharing, referencing, and discussing the meanings of place names across generations that have not been publicly shared or documented.

In writing this monograph, I've presented stories concerning these Anishinaabe toponyms, their preservation, and their visible return to Gaa-waabaabiganikaag. I am incredibly grateful to the Ojibwe people of White Earth who shared their time, knowledge, and experiences with me. I'm especially grateful to Doug McArthur, who initially encouraged me to go drive past these markers back in the summer of 2017. And I'm deeply grateful to Mary Otto, Merlin, and the numerous Anishinaabe language educators who are ensuring that the Ojibwe youth of today become the Anishinaabemowin teachers of the present and the future.

I wish to conclude this Element with an excerpt from Nicollet's journal, recorded on July 29, 1836. The entry for this night tells of the transmission of geographic knowledge – relating to the stars, constellations, and the four directions – between two Ojibwe people, Chagobay and Brunia. These Anishinaabe navigators served as guides for the French geographer. Nicollet paints a scene of observers gazing into the night sky:

> The night was still, the sky full of stars . . . I listened to my Indians, who were talking excitedly, and I asked what they were talking about. Brunia told me that Chagobay was teaching him to recognize the stars. I found room among Chagobay's disciples and he taught me first of all the four cardinal points which are: *Kiou-etten* (north); *Chaouanon* (south); *Qua Banon* (east, the wind of the day); and *Gabé Hen* (west).

Nicollet then "inquired if there were not any other winds," and Chagobay shared "they did not know of any others."[314] This exchange itself required movements between Anishinaabemowin and French, as well as concepts, understandings, and meanings expressed and legible within each (e.g., "winds" and "cardinal points"). Mediation and translation were occurring simultaneously in this lesson and dialogue, with participants navigating speech and spatial worldviews. As Nicollet noted elsewhere in his journal, Brunia had to translate between Anishinaabemowin and French for the benefit of Chagobay and Nicollet, with Nicollet's journal in French later being translated into English by André Ferrey.[315]

On this summer night in 1836, Chagobay communicated knowledge of Ojibwe constellations to Brunia and Nicollet, naming and spatially identifying the animals represented in the lights of the night sky. Chagobay shared

[314] Nicollet (1836/1970, pp. 35–36). [315] Nicollet (1836/1970, pp. v–vii, 52, 73).

constellations including the fisher (*Odgi-ganank*) and the bear's head (*Mascouté-gouan*).[316] Before these navigators went to sleep, Chagobay pointed out "the North Star, *Kiou-batten-nanank*, or the star that does not move as the others do." Brunia (Ojibwe/French), along with their companion William, informed Nicollet that "the natives have their constellations, which they name after animals they know, belonging to their own region."[317]

This lesson recorded by Nicollet demonstrates the intense scale and expanse of Anishinaabe geographic knowledge, while situating this knowledge through locally known presences and relations. Nicollet, in developing one of the most accurate maps of the upper Mississippi River region during this time, was paying close attention to how these Ojibwe navigators articulated, conceptualized, and knew the space surrounding them. This is supported by his commentary on Brunia's contributions to his mapping during this period:

> And I also find time for working on my detailed maps with Brunia. The more I travel with this kind man, the more credit I give to the prodigious memory with which he is gifted and also to his profound knowledge of the land. He is always there to supplement for me the details I overlooked or forgot,

Figure 30 Mashkode Bizhiki Ziibii sign (after sundown). Photo by author.

[316] Note: In Nicollet (1836/1970), translator André Ferrey wrote, "While the substance of the journals caused little problem, botanical phrases and animal identifications were often puzzling – not to say insoluble without the help of those more familiar with the terrain than I. Mrs. Bray and I struggled together with many of the Indian words" (pp. vi–vii).

[317] Nicollet (1836/1970, pp. 35–36).

> supplying such extraordinary deductions and combinations of rivers, lakes, pathways, and portages that their result invariably fits into the pattern of my astronomical observations which are the foundation of the geographical research I am carrying out here.[318]

These passages from Nicollet's journal illustrate how Ojibwe geographic knowledge was not confined by the borders of reservations, but rather by the extent of the navigable and the perceivable.

Reflecting on Nicollet's 1836 travels in 2012, Jim Jones (Leech Lake Band of Ojibwe) described how the routes taken by Chagobay, Brunia, and Nicollet relate to his life: "The history is alive inside of me. It's alive because I know the history of these places and these locations, and this travel route between Crow Wing to Leech Lake." For the same radio series, Andy Favorite, the late White Earth Historian, shared how Anishinaabe people's geographic knowledge and navigation was intimately tied to the rivers and lakes throughout Ojibwe country: "All this stuff is connected. When they would travel in the old days, the highways were the rivers and the roads were the lakes and rivers."[319]

The lakes and rivers of White Earth, as well as off-reservation homewaters, remain places of relationships, memories, and belonging for Ojibwe people. These signs demonstrate that Anishinaabeg of the present – such as Mary Otto and Merlin – are ensuring that Ojibwe youth and people know they belong throughout Gaa-waabaabiganikaag and that their language is alive. They are the inheritors of enduring intergenerational relationships and histories with the waters that surround them at the Land of the White Clay.

---

[318] Nicollet (1836/1970, p. 127).

[319] Northern Community Radio – KAXE & KBXE, "Our History: The Journey of Chagobay and Brunia – Ten-part series," Part 1 (2012).

References

Adler, E. (2023). "Bison Herd Makes a Powerful Return to Shakopee Mdewakanton Sioux Land in the South Metro." *The Minnesota Star Tribune*, December 31. www.startribune.com/bison-herd-makes-a-powerful-return-to-shakopee-mdewakanton-sioux-land-in-the-south-metro/600331229.

Allen, J. (1832). *Map of the Route Passed over by an Expedition into the Indian Country in 1832 to the Source of the Mississippi*. Washington, DC: U.S. War Department. John R. Borchert Map Library at the University of Minnesota. https://umedia.lib.umn.edu/item/p16022coll230:701.

Anishinaabeg Today: A Monthly Chronicle of the White Earth Nation. (2016). "A New 'Sign' of the Times . . . ." November 2, 2016. P. 1. https://whiteearth.com/assets/files/newspaper/2016/nov02.pdf.

Anishinaabeg Today: A Monthly Chronicle of White Earth Nation. (2021). "News from Chairman Michael Fairbanks." August 4. P. 3. https://whiteearth.com/assets/files/newspaper/2021/August%204,%202021%20c.pdf.

Anishinaabeg Today: A Monthly Chronicle of White Earth Nation (2022). "News from Chairman Michael Fairbanks." March 2. P. 9. https://whiteearth.com/assets/files/newspaper/2022/March%202,%202022%20c.pdf.

Anishinaabeg Today: A Monthly Chronicle of the White Earth Nation. (2024). "WE Bison Program continues to move forward." November 6. P. 7, www.whiteearth.com/media/pages/community/anishinaabeg-today/04abbae3a4-1731450469/november-6-2024-c.pdf.

"Anthropologic Miscellanea" (Rev. Gilfillan Obituary). (1913). *American Anthropologist* **15**(4), 712–713. https://archive.org/details/sim_american-anthropologist_october-december-1913_15_4/page/712/.

Barnd, N. B. (2017). *Native Space: Geographic Strategies to Unsettle Settler Colonialism*. Portland: Oregon State University Press.

Beaulieu, G. H. (1907). "Buffalo Killed at White Earth." In A. H. Wilcox and J. C. West, eds., *Pioneer History of Becker County, Minnesota*. Saint Paul, MN: Pioneer Press Company, pp. 54–55. www.loc.gov/item/17012304/.

Beltrami, G. C. (1827). *Map of the Mississippi River from Lake Winnipeg to the Gulf of Mexico*. London: Hunter and Clarke. John R. Borchert Map Library at the University of Minnesota. https://umedia.lib.umn.edu/item/p16022coll230:4484.

Beltrami, G. C. (1828). *A Pilgrimage in Europe and America, Leading to the Discovery of the Sources of the Mississippi and Bloody River, Vol. 2*. London: Hunt and Clark. https://archive.org/details/pilgrimageineuro02beltuoft/.

Benton-Banai, E. (1988/2010). *The Mishomis Book: The Voice of the Ojibway*. Minneapolis: University of Minnesota Press.

Calloway, C. G. (2004). *First Peoples: A Documentary Survey of American Indian History, 2nd Ed*. Boston, MA: Bedford/St. Martin's.

Child, B. (1998). *Boarding School Seasons: American Indian Families, 1900–1940*. Lincoln: University of Nebraska Press.

Child, B. (2012). *Holding Our World Together: Ojibwe Women and the Survival of Community*. New York: Penguin Books.

Clouston, R. (1846). *Sketch of Journey between R.R.S. and St. Peter's in United States – 1846*. In *Robert Clouston Narratives, 1846, 1850*. Minnesota Historical Society. Saint Paul, MN. https://mnpals-mhs.primo.exlibrisgroup.com/permalink/01MNPALS_MHS/ge68j0/alma990017181070104294.

Cole, D. G. and Hart, E. R. (2021). "The Importance of Indigenous Cartography and Toponymy to Historical Land Tenure and Contributions to Euro/American/Canadian Cartography." *International Journal of Geo-Information* **10**(6), 397. https://doi.org/10.3390/ijgi10060397.

Coulthard, G. (2014). *Red Skin, White Masks: Rejecting the Colonial Politics of Recognition*. Minneapolis: University of Minnesota Press.

Crane, E. (1947). "White Men's Dull Names Make Poetic Indians Very Unhappy." *Minneapolis Tribune*, March 16, 1947. In "Society Records, 1944–1959" of the Ojibway-Dakota Research Society of Minnesota, Folder 1, Minnesota Historical Society, Saint Paul, MN.

De Rosa, M. (2010). "Letters from the Mackinaw Mission School." *The New England Quarterly* **83**(4), 705–718.

Densmore, F. (1910). *Chippewa Music*. In Bureau of American Ethnology, Smithsonian Institution, Bulletin 45. Washington, DC: Government Printing Office. https://archive.org/details/chippewamusic00dens/.

Doerfler, J. (2015). *Those Who Belong: Identity, Family, Blood, and Citizenship among the White Earth Anishinaabeg*. East Lansing: Michigan State University Press.

Erdrich, H. (2013). "'Name': Literary Ancestry as Presence". In J. Doerfler, N. J. Sinclair, and H. K. Stark, eds., *Centering Anishinaabeg Studies: Understanding the World through Stories*. East Lansing: Michigan State University Press, pp. 13–34.

Garrioch, P. (1844). *Peter Garrioch Diaries, 1837, 1843–1847*. Minnesota Historical Society. Saint Paul, MN. https://mnpals-mhs.primo.exlibrisgroup.com/permalink/01MNPALS_MHS/ge68j0/alma990017303440104294.

Gidigaa Migizi (Williams, D.). (2018). *Michi Saagiig Nishnaabeg: This Is Our Territory*. Winnipeg: Arbeiter Ring.

Rev. Gilfillan, J. A. (1885). "Minnesota Geographical Names Derived from the Chippewa Language." Submitted to the Minnesota Historical Society on April 13, 1885. In N. H. Winchell, ed., *The Geological and Natural History Survey of Minnesota: The Thirteenth Annual Report, for the Year 1884*. Saint Paul: Pioneer Press Company, pp. 451–477. www.google.com/books/edition/The_Annual_Report_for_the_Year/6tdLAAAAMAAJ.

Gilman, R. R., Gilman, C., and Stultz, D. M. (1979). *The Red River Trails: Oxcart Routes Between St. Paul and the Selkirk Settlement, 1820–1870*. Saint Paul: Minnesota Historical Society.

Goeman, M. (2013). *Mark My Words: Native Women Mapping Our Nations*. Minneapolis: University of Minnesota Press.

Gross, L. W. (2014). *Anishinaabe Ways of Knowing and Being*. London: Routledge.

Gudmundson, W. (2018). *White Earth Window*. Catalogue and Exhibit, Nemeth Art Center, July 1–28. www.nemethartcenter.org/past/wayne-gudmundson.

Henry, G. (2019). "(Chapter 9) Re-incurating Tribal Skins: Re-imagining the Native Archive, Re-stor(y)ing the Tribal Imagi(Native)." In I. Schweitzer and G. Henry, eds., *Afterlives of Indigenous Archives: Essays in Honor of The Occom Circle*. Hanover, NH: Dartmouth College Press, pp. 172–188.

Hind, H. Y. (1860). *Narrative of the Canadian Red River Exploring Expedition of 1857 and of the Assinniboine and Saskatchewan Exploring Expedition of 1858*. London: Longman, Green, Longman, and Roberts. https://archive.org/details/narrativeofcanad11860hind/.

Jacoby, K. (2003). *Crimes against Nature: Squatters, Poachers, Thieves, and the Hidden History of American Conservation*. Berkeley: University of California Press.

Kemper, J., Breck, J. L., Manney, S. W. et al. (1858). "The Indian Races in America." May 14, 1858. In *The Colonial Church Chronicle and Missionary Journal*, pp. 800–804. https://archive.org/details/colonialchurchc02unkngoog/page/802/.

Kimmerer, R. W. (2013). *Braiding Sweetgrass: Indigenous Wisdom, Scientific Knowledge, and the Teachings of Plants*. Canada: Milkweed Editions.

Kimmerer, R. W. (2017). "(Chapter 26) The Covenant of Reciprocity." In J. Hart, ed., *The Wiley Blackwell Companion to Religion and Ecology*. Hoboken, NJ: John Wiley & Sons, pp. 368–381.

Kraker, D. (2024). "Grand Portage Band and MnDOT to unveil Ojibwe-English Road Signs." *Minnesota Public Radio*, May 12. www.mprnews.org/story/2024/05/12/grand-portage-band-and-mndot-to-unveil-ojibweenglish-road-signs.

LaDuke, W. (1993). “Voices from White Earth: Gaa-waabaabiganikaag.” Thirteenth Annual E. F. Shumacher Lectures, October. New Haven, CT. https://centerforneweconomics.org/publications/voices-from-white-earth-gaa-waabaabiganikaag/.

LaDuke, W. (1999). *All Our Relations: Native Struggles for Land and Life*. Cambridge, MA: South End Press.

Madison, W. (1957). Letter from William Madison (Ojibway-Dakota Research Society) to Russell Fridley (Minnesota Historical Society), December 7, 1957. In “Society Records, 1944–1959” of the Ojibway-Dakota Research Society of Minnesota, Folder 1, Minnesota Historical Society, Saint Paul, MN.

Mason, P. P. (ed.). (1993). “Appendix C: Journal and Letters of Lieutenant James Allen.” In *Schoolcraft's Expedition to Lake Itasca*. East Lansing: Michigan State University Press, pp. 163–241.

Mayfield, P. (2016). “White Earth Asks for Ojibwe on Lake Signs.” *DL-Online /Detroit Lakes Tribune*, January 10. www.dl-online.com/news/white-earth-asks-for-ojibwe-on-lake-signs.

McDougall, Leonard Sonny. (n.d.) “Ojibwe Word Parts & Definitions.” Minnesota Department of Transportation (MnDOT). www.dot.state.mn.us/mntribes/pdf/ojibwe-word-parts-definitions.pdf.

Meyer, M. L. (1991). “‘We Can Not Get a Living as We Used To’: Dispossession and the White Earth Anishinaabeg, 1889–1920.” *The American Historical Review* **96**(2), 368–394.

Meyer, M. L. (1999). *The White Earth Tragedy: Ethnicity and Dispossession at a Minnesota Anishinaabe Reservation, 1889–1920*. Lincoln: University of Nebraska Press.

Minnesota Chippewa Tribe. (1936). “Constitution and Bylaws of the Minnesota Chippewa Tribe.” Office of Indian Affairs, Department of the Interior, United States. Approved July 24. Washington, DC: Government Printing Office. https://mnchippewatribe.com/pdf/1936%20Constitution.pdf.

Minnesota Department of Transportation (MnDOT). (n.d.). “Dakota and Ojibwe Language Signing Program.” https://web.archive.org/web/20170822021401/https://www.dot.state.mn.us/trafficeng/signing/docs/dakotaorojibwelanguagesigningprogram.pdf.

Minnesota Department of Transportation (MnDOT). (n.d.). “Ojibwe Sign Translations.” Accessed June 3, 2020. www.dot.state.mn.us/mntribes/pdf/ojibwe-sign-translations.xlsx.

Minnesota Historical Society. (1944). “General Minnesota Items.” *Minnesota History* **25**(3), 304. https://archive.org/details/sim_minnesota-history_1944-09_25_3/page/304/.

Minnesota Historical Society. (1947). "News from the States." *Minnesota History* **28**(4), 374. https://archive.org/details/sim_minnesota-history_1947-12_28_4/page/374/.

Minnesota Historical Society. (n.d.). "The Progress." Accessed January 10, 2025. www.mnhs.org/newspapers/hub/progress.

Minnesota Historical Society. (n.d.). "The Tomahawk." Accessed January 10, 2025. www.mnhs.org/newspapers/hub/tomahawk.

Minnesota Pollution Control Agency. (n.d.). "Otter Tail River." Accessed January 13, 2025. www.pca.state.mn.us/watershed-information/otter-tail-river.

Minnesota Supreme Court. (1977). *State* v. *Zay Zah*, 259 N.W 2. 580. https://law.justia.com/cases/minnesota/supreme-court/1977/46834-1.html.

MnDOT Newsline. (2016). "District 4 Teams with White Earth Reservation to Place Ojibwe and English Language Signs." September 21. www.newsline.dot.state.mn.us/archive/16/Sept/21.html.

Molin, P. F. (1983). "Foreword" in *Night Flying Woman: An Ojibway Narrative*, by Ignatia Broker. Saint Paul: Borealis Books/Minnesota Historical Society Press.

National Public Radio. (2017). "Why Treaties Matter | NPR." YouTube video. November 22. 01:35–01:57. www.youtube.com/watch?v=bexvE4lZRGo.

Nicollet, J. N. (1836/1970). *The Journals of Joseph N. Nicollet: A Scientist on the Mississippi Headwaters with Notes on Indian Life, 1836–37*. Trans. André Ferrey, ed. Martha Coleman Bray. Saint Paul: Minnesota Historical Society. Translation published in 1970. https://archive.org/details/journalsofjoseph0000nico/.

Nicollet, J. N. (1843). *Report Intended to Illustrate a Map of the Hydrographical Basin of the Upper Mississippi River, February 16, 1841*. United States Senate, 26th Congress, 2d Session. Washington, DC: Blair and Rives, Printers. www.loc.gov/item/rc01001193/.

Nicollet, J. N., Frémont, J. C., Emory, W. H., and Abert, J. J. (1843). *Hydrographical Basin of the Upper Mississippi River from Astronomical and Barometrical Observations, Surveys, and Information*. Washington, DC: G. Graham Lith. University of Michigan, Clark Library. https://quod.lib.umich.edu/c/clark1ic/x-003283294/39015091905888.

Norrgard, C. (2014). *Seasons of Change: Labor, Treaty Rights, and Ojibwe Nationhood*. Chapel Hill: University of North Carolina Press.

Northern Community Radio – KAXE & KBXE. (2012). "Our History: The Journey of Chagobay and Brunia – Ten-part series" (Part 1). August 18. 02:40–2:56, 05:53–06:10. https://ampers.org/our-history-the-journey-of-chagobay-and-brunia-ten-part-series/.

Northern Community Radio – KAXE & KBXE. (2012). "Our History: The Journey of Chagobay and Brunia – Ten-part series" (Part 7). August 18. 01:29–01:57, 05:01–05:58.

Northern Community Radio – KAXE & KBXE. (2012). "Our History: The Journey of Chagobay and Brunia – Ten-part series" (Part 10). August 18. 01:05–01:27.

O'Brien, J. M. (2010). *Firsting and Lasting: Writing Indians Out of Existence in New England*. Minneapolis: University of Minnesota Press.

O'Brien, J. M. (2017). "Presidential Address: Memory and Mobility: Grandma's Mahnomen, White Earth." *Ethnohistory* **64**(3), 345–377.

Ogimaa Mikana Project. (2013–2025). "Ogimaa Mikana: Reclaiming/Renaming." Tumblr. https://ogimaamikana.tumblr.com/.

The Ogimaa Mikana Collective: Blight, S., King, H., Pion, C. et al. (2014). "The Ogimaa Mikana Project." In The Kino-nda-niimi Collective, ed., *The Winter We Danced: Voices from the Past, the Future, and the Idle No More Movement*. Winnipeg: ARP Books, 329–332.

Ojibway Research Society of Minnesota. (1944). *Report No. 1: Ojibway Names of Some Northern Minnesota Lakes*. April 1. Minneapolis, MN. In "Society Records, 1944–1959" of the Ojibway-Dakota Research Society of Minnesota, Folder 2, Minnesota Historical Society, Saint Paul, MN.

Ojibway-Dakota Research Society of Minnesota. (1945). *Report No. 2: Ojibway and Dakota Names of Some Minnesota Lakes, Rivers, Other Natural Features and Settlements*. December 1. Minneapolis, MN. In "Society Records, 1944–1959" of the Ojibway-Dakota Research Society of Minnesota, Folder 3, Minnesota Historical Society, Saint Paul, MN.

Ojibway-Dakota Research Society of Minnesota. (n.d.). *Report No. 4*. Date Unknown. Minneapolis MN. In "Society Records, 1944–1959" of the Ojibway-Dakota Research Society of Minnesota, Folder 6, Minnesota Historical Society, Saint Paul, MN.

Ojibway-Dakota Research Society of Minnesota. (n.d.). *Report No. 5*. Date Unknown. Minneapolis MN. In "Society Records, 1944–1959" of the Ojibway-Dakota Research Society of Minnesota, Folder 7, Minnesota Historical Society, Saint Paul, MN.

Ojibway-Dakota Research Society of Minnesota. (1950). *Report No. 6*. Minneapolis, MN. In "Society Records, 1944–1959" of the Ojibway-Dakota Research Society of Minnesota, Folder 8, Minnesota Historical Society, Saint Paul, MN.

Ojibway-Dakota Research Society of Minnesota. (1963). "Ojibway and Dakota Place Names in Minnesota," ed. Karen Daniels Petersen. *The Minnesota Archaeologist* **25**(1), 5–40. www.dot.state.mn.us/trafficeng/signing/docs/mn-archaeologist-place-names.pdf.

Olson, M. (2023). "Bison herd helps restore Prairie Island community." *Minnesota Public Radio News*, December 8. www.mprnews.org/story/2023/12/08/bison-herd-helps-restore-prairie-island-community.

Pochedley, E. (2021). "Restorative Cartography of the Theakiki Region: Mapping Potawatomi Presences in Indiana." *Open Rivers: Rethinking Water, Place & Community* **18**. https://doi.org/10.24926/2471190X.7923.

Povinelli, E. A. (2002). *The Cunning of Recognition: Indigenous Alterities and the Making of Australian Multiculturalism*. Durham: Duke University Press.

Prairie Island Indian Community. (n.d.). "Edwin Buck Jr. Memorial Buffalo Project." https://prairieisland.org/who-we-are/our-culture/buffalo-project.

Pyle, K. (2020). "(Chapter 5) Reclaiming Traditional Gender Roles: A Two-Spirit Critique." In S. Nickel and A. Fehr, eds., *In Good Relation: History, Gender, and Kinship in Indigenous Feminisms*. Winnipeg: University of Manitoba Press, pp. 109–122.

"Ratified Indian Treaty 251: Chippewa (Pillager Band) – Leech Lake, August 21, 1847." (1847). National Archives Catalog. https://catalog.archives.gov/id/174680021.

Redix, E. M. (2014). *The Murder of Joe White: Ojibwe Leadership and Colonialism in Wisconsin*. East Lansing: Michigan State University Press.

Redix, E. M. (2024). "Rivers of Lake Superior's North Shore: Historical Methodology and Ojibwe Dialects." *Open Rivers: Rethinking Water, Place & Community* **26**. https://doi.org/10.24926/2471190X.11360.

Redix, E. M., Cochrane, T., Jourdain, G., Zimmerman Jr., M., and Swingen, M. (n.d.). "Rivers of the North Shore." *Ojibwe.net*. https://ojibwe.net/rivers-of-the-north-shore/.

Rice, W. (2020). "Ogimaa Mikana Project Uses Language to Reclaim Roads and Landmarks of Anishinaabe Territory." *CBC News*, March 5. www.cbc.ca/news/canada/sudbury/living-languages-susan-blight-ogimaa-mikana-public-art-project-street-signs-billboards-1.5485914.

Ross, J. (2016). "White Earth Band Wants Road Signs to Reflect Ojibwe Language." *The Minnesota Star Tribune*, January 24. www.startribune.com/tribe-wants-road-signs-to-reflect-ojibwe-language/366314401/.

Schaaf, W. and Robertson, C. (1978). *History of the Minnesota Chippewa Tribe*. Minnesota Chippewa Tribe Curriculum Development Staff. https://static1.squarespace.com/static/58901f76d482e91a3029c006/t/594ec38120099e6f69bf430c/1498334115294/HistoryofMCT_1978.pdf.

Schultz, J. (1894). *The Old Crow Wing Trail*. Winnipeg: Manitoba Free Press Print. https://archive.org/details/trent_0116402015824/.

Shoemaker, N. (1988). "Urban Indians and Ethnic Choices: American Indian Organizations in Minneapolis, 1920–1950." *Western Historical Quarterly* **19** (4), 431–447.

Simpson, A. (2014). *Mohawk Interruptus: Political Life across the Borders of Settler States*. Durham, NC: Duke University Press.

Simpson, L. B. (2011). *Dancing on Our Turtle's Back: Stories of Nishnaabeg Re-creation, Resurgence and a New Emergence*. Winnipeg: Arbeiter Ring.

Simpson, L. B. (2017). *As We Have Always Done: Indigenous Freedom Through Radical Resistance*. Minneapolis: University of Minnesota Press.

Spears, J. A. W. (1907). "History of White Earth." In A. H. Wilcox and J. C. West, eds., *Pioneer History of Becker County, Minnesota*. Saint Paul, MN: Pioneer Press Company, pp. 246–264. www.loc.gov/item/17012304/.

Stark, H. K and Stark, K. J. (2018). "Nenabozho Goes Fishing: A Sovereignty Story." *Daedalus* **147**(2), 17–26.

The Tomahawk. (1903). "Indians Will Celebrate." July 2, vol. 1, no. 14. P. 4. www.mnhs.org/newspapers/lccn/sn89064695/1903-07-02/ed-1/seq-4.

The Tomahawk. (June 1916). "Delegates to the Bemidji Council." June 22, vol. XIV, no. 9. P. 1. www.mnhs.org/newspapers/lccn/sn89064695/1916-06-22/ed-1/seq-1.

The Tomahawk. (December 1916). "News of White Earth and Vicinity." December 7, vol. XIV, no. 33. P. 8. www.mnhs.org/newspapers/lccn/sn89064695/1916-12-07/ed-1/seq-8.

The Tomahawk. (1920). "Local Council Elects Delegates." June 3, vol. XVIII, no. 7. P. 1. www.mnhs.org/newspapers/lccn/sn89064695/1920-06-03/ed-1/seq-1.

The Tomahawk. (1921). "Gets Poor Reception at Pine Point." June 30, vol. XVIIII, no. 10. P. 4. www.mnhs.org/newspapers/lccn/sn89064695/1921-06-30/ed-1/seq-4.

"Treaty with the Sioux, etc., 1825." (1825). August 19. Tribal Treaties Database. https://treaties.okstate.edu/treaties/treaty-with-the-sioux-etc-1825-0250.

Treuer, A. S. (2010). *Ojibwe in Minnesota*. Saint Paul: Minnesota Historical Society Press.

U.S. Congress. (1912). "White Earth Reservation: Hearings before a Subcommittee of the Committee on Expenditures in the Interior Department of the House of Representatives on House Resolution No. 103 to Investigate the Expenditures in the Interior Department." February 2–17. Washington, DC: Government Printing Office, 925–1760. https://archive.org/details/whiteearthreser00depagoog/.

U.S. Office of Indian Affairs. (1867). "Agency of the Chippewas of the Mississippi and Others." In *Annual Report on Indian Affairs, by the Acting*

Commissioner, Office of Indian Affairs, Department of the Interior, November 15, p. 24. https://digitalcommons.law.ou.edu/indianserialset/5621/.

U.S. War Department, Allen, J., and Schoolcraft, H. R. (1834). *Schoolcraft and Allen–Expedition to Northwest Indians: Letter from the Secretary of War, Transmitting a Map and Report of Lieut. Allen and H.B. Schoolcraft's Visit to the Northwest Indians in 1832*. April 12. Washington, DC: Gales and Seaton. www.loc.gov/item/08033593/.

University of Minnesota Morris. (n.d.). "Molin Collection." https://library.morris.umn.edu/collections/molin-collection.

Upham, W. (1920). *Minnesota Geographic Names: Their Origin and Historic Significance*. In *Collections of the Minnesota Historical Society, Volume XVII.* Saint Paul: Minnesota Historical Society.

Vannote, V. and Pratt, J. (1999). *Women of White Earth*. Minneapolis: University of Minnesota Press. https://archive.org/details/womenofwhiteeart00vann.

Rev. Verwyst, C. (1916). "*A Glossary of Chippewa Indian Names of Rivers Lakes, and Villages*, Acta et Dicta, vol. 4, no. 2, pp. 253–274, July 1916." Call Number BX940. A2 v.4:2. Minnesota Historical Society Collections.

Vizenor, G. R. (2009). *Native Liberty: Natural Reason and Cultural Survivance*. Lincoln: University of Nebraska Press.

Wakefield, J. B. (1906). "First Land Plowed in Becker County." Letter – Aitkin, Minn., July 22, 1906. In A. H. Wilcox and J. C. West, eds., *Pioneer History of Becker County, Minnesota*. Saint Paul, MN: Pioneer Press, pp. 240–241. www.loc.gov/item/17012304/.

Rev. Watrin, B. (1930). *The Ponsfordian: 1880–1930*. Park Rapids: Press of The Park Rapids Enterprise. https://archive.org/details/ponsfordian188010 0watr/.

WCCO CBS News Minnesota. (2023). "Bison to Roam Tribal Land Near Shakopee This Fall." July 27. www.cbsnews.com/minnesota/news/shakopee-mdewakanton-sioux-community-bison-dakota/.

Whetung, M. (2016). "Doing Indigenous Geography." In *Nishnaabeg Encounters: Living Indigenous Landscapes*. Master's thesis, University of Toronto, pp. 90–111. https://tspace.library.utoronto.ca/bitstream/1807/76189/3/Whetung_Madeline_201611_MA_thesis.pdf.

White Earth Nation. (n.d.) "Natural Resources." https://web.archive.org/web/20240328231837/https://whiteearth.com/divisions/natural_resources/services.

White Earth Reservation Curriculum Committee, Gawboy, C., Goodwin, D., and Premo, S. (1989). *White Earth: A History*. Cass Lake: Minnesota Chippewa Tribe. https://whiteearth.com/assets/files/culture/White_Earth_A_History.pdf https://search.worldcat.org/en/title/20621244.

Whyte, K. (2017). "The Dakota Access Pipeline, Environmental Injustice, and US Colonialism." *Red Ink: An International Journal of Indigenous Literature, Arts, & Humanities* **19**(1), 154–169.

Whyte, K. (2018). "Settler Colonialism, Ecology, and Environmental Injustice." *Environment and Society: Advances in Research* **9**, 125–144.

Wierima, B. (2011). "Paranormal in Pine Point." *DL-Online/Detroit Lakes Tribune*, October 19. www.dl-online.com/news/paranormal-in-pine-point.

Wilcox, A. H. (1907). *Pioneer History of Becker County, Minnesota*. Eds. A. H. Wilcox and J. C. West. Saint Paul, MN: Pioneer Press. www.loc.gov/item/17012304/.

Wilkins, D. E. (ed.). (2019). *Documents of Native American Political Development: 1933 to Present*. Oxford: Oxford University Press.

Witgen, M. (2011). *An Infinity of Nations: How the Native New World Shaped Early North America*. Philadelphia: University of Pennsylvania Press.

WTIP North Shore Community Radio and Media. (2024). "Erik Redix on Ojibwe River Names Project." YouTube video. May 22. https://youtu.be/y-X1341sjPM?si=-VhldCI-lrAOc62B.

Acknowledgments

I am deeply grateful to the Ojibwe people of Gaa-waabaabiganikaag for welcoming me into their community and for taking the time to support this research by generously sharing their knowledge. I am thankful to the White Earth Nation citizens, descendants, and personnel quoted and referenced throughout this Element, as well as those who participated in interviews not featured in this specific work.

This Element has been published with the permission of the White Earth Nation Research Review Board (WEN RRB). The author extends his gratitude to the WEN RRB. Ethnographic interviews and fieldwork with White Earth Nation citizens, descendants, and personnel featured throughout this Element were conducted with the approval of the WEN RRB. Permission to conduct this research within the White Earth Reservation was granted by the WEN RRB on June 27, 2017 and July 30, 2019, with a modification for conducting virtual/phone interviews during the COVID-19 pandemic approved on September 1, 2020. Approval to conduct ethnographic research with citizens, descendants, and personnel of the White Earth Nation was also granted by the University of Minnesota Institutional Review Board (UMN IRB) under STUDY00000204 (2017), STUDY00007761 (2019), and MOD00019727 (2020). This research and associated writing have been supported by the National Science Foundation Graduate Research Fellowship Program (NSF GRFP), the DOVE Summer Research Fellowship through the University of Minnesota, the Charles Eastman Fellowship at Dartmouth College, and the 1855 Professorship in Great Lakes Anishinaabe Knowledge, Spiritualities, and Cultural Practices at Michigan State University. **NSF GRFP Disclaimer**: "This material is based upon work supported by the National Science Foundation Graduate Research Fellowship Program under Grant No. 1839286. Any opinions, findings, and conclusions or recommendations expressed in this material are those of the author and do not necessarily reflect the views of the National Science Foundation." To reiterate, the author's findings and conclusions are his own and do not necessarily reflect the views of any of the aforementioned research review boards, fellowships, positions, or associated institutions/governments.

I wish to recognize Dr. Carson Gardner, the former chair of the WEN RRB, who walked on before this Element was completed. I am profoundly thankful for all of his support with my research at White Earth and for his always uplifting messages on the significance of this work. In an article featured in the February 7, 2024 edition of *Anishinaabeg Today*, Dr. Gardner addressed why it is important for the White Earth Nation to have a Research Review Board, writing the following: "Why let anybody do research here at all? Because Gaa-waabaabiganikaag has beautiful, practical, Anishinaabe lifeways and good Anishinaabe healing knowledge to share, to help all human beings and to help protect land, water, sky, inner fire, language, true history, creatures, and to respect helping spirits." Chi-miigwech Dr. Gardner and the WEN RRB for allowing me to conduct this research on Ojibwe geographic knowledge, belonging to place, environmental obligations, histories, and the revitalization of Anishinaabemowin.

I wish to thank Dr. Jean O'Brien, Dr. Hoon Song, Dr. Katherine Hayes, Dr. Jill Doerfler, Dr. Kevin Murphy, Dr. David Chang, Dr. Brenda Child, and Dr. David Valentine. These mentors, teachers, and scholars encouraged the development of an earlier version of this work, created space to formulate and workshop this writing, and offered invaluable feedback. I thank Dr. Rose Miron and Dr. Sasha Suarez for offering thoughtful comments on an early draft during our time as graduate students at the University of Minnesota. This work has benefited from discussions with colleagues from the Department of Religious Studies and the American Indian & Indigenous Studies (AIIS) program at Michigan State University. I am especially grateful to Dr. Amy DeRogatis and Dr. Kristin Arola for their support during the process of writing and revising this Element. Finally, I thank Dr. Caroline Doenmez and Dr. Blaire Morseau for their much-needed help in condensing Section 5, "Roots in White Clay: A Pre-Reservation History of Gaa-waabaabiganikaag," as well as their steadfast encouragement and generosity.

This Element is dedicated to the Anishinaabeg of Gaa-waabaabiganikaag, the Ojibwe of White Earth.

Cambridge Elements

Indigenous Environmental Research

presence in historical sources such as maps and treaties, and in reconnecting Indigenous collections in museums with their source communities. He co-leads the "Green Toolkit for a New Space Economy" project, which aims to widen the space sector's understanding of sustainability to include the cultural and social dimensions. His collaborators include King's Digital Lab at King's College London, The Alan Turing Institute, and Nordamerika Native Museum Zurich. His research interests are on the process of meaning-making, particularly in understanding senses of time and place, and on the repercussions of trauma and disruption. His research on early modern futurity has been published in *Historical Research*, and he teaches courses on cultural astronomy, public history, and digital history.

About the Series

Elements in Indigenous Environmental Research offers state-of-the-art interdisciplinary analyses within the rapidly growing area of Indigenous environmental research. The series investigates how environmental issues and processes relate to Indigenous socio-economic, cultural and political dynamics.

Cambridge Elements

Elements in Indigenous Environmental Research

Elements in the Series

Defending Community, Territory, and Indigenous Environmental Relations
Levi Gahman, Filiberto Penados, Cristina Coc and Shelda-Jane Smith

"Alaska" Is Not a Blank Space: Unsettling Aldo Leopold's Odyssey
Julianne Warren

Indigenous Rights to Land Versus Extractivism: The Promise and Limits of ILO Convention No. 169 in Mexico
Tamara A. Wattnem

The Rediscovery of Huaca Pintada: Why Traditional Ecological Knowledge Matters Within Archaeological Environments in Peru
Sâm Ghavami and Christian Cancho Ruiz

Restoring Indigenous Place Names: Making Anishinaabe Toponyms Visible Throughout the White Earth Ojibwe Reservation
Elan Pochedley

A full series listing is available at: www.cambridge.org/EIER

Printed by Integrated Books International,
United States of America